MOVE IT!

STUDENTS' BOOK

FIONA BEDDALL AND JAYNE WILDMAN

SERIES CONSULTANT: CARA NORRIS-RAMIREZ

Unit	Page	Grammar	Vocabulary
5 **Enjoy Your Vacation!** ❑ **Literature File**	4	Present perfect + *for* and *since*; *How long?* Past simple with *just*	Vacation Meanings of *get*
6 **That's Life!** ❑ **Real World Profiles**	14	*Have to/Don't have to; Must/ Mustn't* Predictions with *will, won't, might*	Household chores Feelings adjectives
Review 2 Units 4–6	24		
7 **Make a Difference** ❑ **Global Citizenship File**	28	*Be going to* and *will* First conditional	Protest and support Verb + preposition
8 **Danger and Risk** ❑ **Real World Profiles**	38	Second conditional Relative pronouns	Extreme adjectives Illness and injury
9 **Inventions** ❑ **Science File**	48	Present simple passive Past simple passive	Machine nouns and verbs Word building
Review 3 Units 7–9	58		
Brain Trainers	62		
Listening Bank	66		
Culture	68		

Reading and Listening	Speaking and Pronunciation	Writing
Behind the Camera Strange Tourist Attractions Radio interview Dictation	Asking for information **Pronunciation:** /aɪ/ vs /ɪ/	A travel guide **Writing File:** Making your writing more interesting
Today's Teens Don't Do Chores Future Teens Teenagers of the future Dictation	Giving advice **Pronunciation:** /ʌ/ and /yu/	A problem page **Writing File:** Linking words: reason and result
Dana Point Elephant Parade Do Something Different … An interview about a charity Dictation	Persuading **Pronunciation:** *going to*	A formal letter **Writing File:** Letter writing
Interview: Naomi Daniels Why Are People Risk-Takers? Talking about a TV show Dictation	Talking about health **Pronunciation:** *gh*	An application form **Writing File:** Completing an application form
Teenage Inventors A Book for All Time? Reading stories on a smart phone Dictation	Problems with machines **Pronunciation:** /ɪ/ and /i/	An opinion essay **Writing File:** How to write an opinion essay

Enjoy Your Vacation!

Grammar
Present perfect + *for* and *since*; *How long?*; Past simple with *just*

Vocabulary
Vacation;
Meanings of *get*

Speaking
Asking for information

Writing
A travel guide

Word list page 27
Workbook page 128

Vocabulary • Vacation

1 2.15 **Match the pictures (1–14) to these activities. Then listen, check and repeat.**

book a flight/hotel *1*	buy souvenirs	check into a hotel	eat out
get a tan	get lost	go camping	go sightseeing
lose your luggage	pack your bag	put up a tent	stay in a hotel
take a trip	write a travel blog		

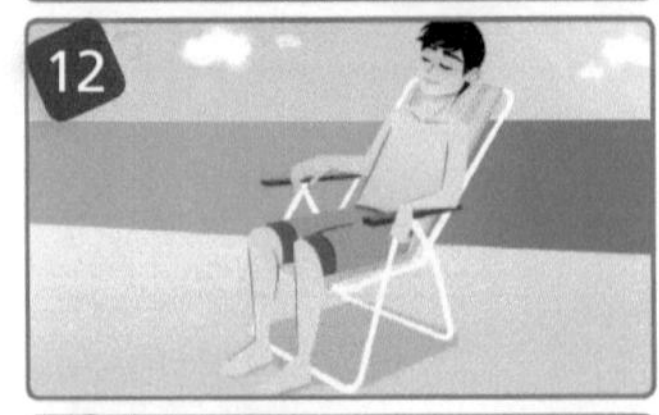

2 Match the sentences to the activities in Exercise 1.

1 We have flights and we've paid for the hotel—I think that's everything. *book a flight/hotel*
2 All the other bags came off the plane, but mine wasn't there!
3 This pink T-shirt is great. It says "I Love NY."
4 I've almost finished, but the bag is really heavy!
5 I want to see the famous cathedral.
6 Let's go to the restaurant by the beach tonight!
7 I'm not sure how to get back to the hotel!

3 Match the verbs (1–6) to the nouns (a–f) to make activities from Exercise 1.

1 stay	a into a hotel
2 write	b a tan
3 go	c a tent
4 check	d a travel blog
5 get	e in a hotel
6 put up	f camping

4 What about you? In pairs, ask and answer.

1 Where do you usually stay when you go on vacation?
2 What do you enjoy doing? Do you like getting a tan or going sightseeing?
3 Have you ever written a travel blog?

I usually stay in a hotel.

Brain Trainer Unit 5
Activity 2
Go to page 62

Reading

1 Look at the photos from Shannon and Jenna's vacation. Answer the questions.

1 What type of vacation is it?
2 Where do you think they are staying?
3 What do you think they do every day?

2 Read the magazine article quickly and check your answers to Exercise 1. Which activity in the photos have Shannon and Jenna not done?

3 Read the article again. Answer the questions.

2.16

Who …

1 likes staying in hotels? *Shannon*
2 likes doing different activities?
3 has never planned a vacation before?
4 has never stayed in a tent before?
5 usually reads books on vacation?
6 has enjoyed the vacation?

4 What about you? In pairs, ask and answer.

1 What do your parents like to do on vacation? Do you like the same things or different things?
2 What are the advantages of a family vacation? Are there any disadvantages?

Advantages
Stay in a nice hotel.
Parents pay for everything.

Disadvantages
Can't stay up late.
Difficult to meet other teenagers.

BEHIND THE CAMERA

People have different ideas about what makes a good vacation, especially parents and their children. In a new TV show, *You Choose!*, kids decide on the family vacation, with some funny results! This week, 16-year-old Jenna Roberts packs the bags and chooses the destination. Her mom, Shannon, gets a big surprise. We asked them about their experiences.

"I think Mom liked canoeing …"

Jenna's story

Mom has always decided where to go on vacation since I was little. We usually stay in hotels, and Mom just likes getting a tan or she reads books all day. I don't mind swimming or listening to my MP3 player, but I like adventure too, so I chose a vacation at the lake. No hotels, no swimming pools, just a tent in a campground (Mom has never put up a tent before). How long have we been here? Mom says "forever!," but actually we've been here for five days. We've tried mountain biking, rock climbing and canoeing since last weekend. Mom was scared on the rock climb, but I think she liked canoeing …

Shannon's story

I was worried when Jenna chose our vacation. I like to relax and read when I'm away, but Jenna is really active. She gets bored easily. It hasn't been a great vacation because I haven't read a book since Saturday. In fact, I haven't read anything for a whole week, but I've had some time to talk to Jenna. That's been the best part, really. We're both too busy to talk at home!

Grammar • Present perfect + *for* and *since*; *How long?*

How long have we been here? We've been here for five days/a week/a month.
I haven't read a book since Saturday.
She's lived in Philadelphia since 2010.

Grammar reference page 118

1 **Study the grammar table. Choose the correct options to complete the rules.**

1 We use *for / since* with a period of time.

2 We use *for / since* with a point in time.

2 **Copy the table and put these words and phrases in the correct column.**

~~a long time~~	~~August~~	a week
five o'clock	four years	I was fifteen
last week	last weekend	ten minutes
Tuesday	two days	yesterday

for	since
a long time	August

3 **Make sentences with the Present perfect. Add *for* or *since* to each sentence.**

1 They / be on / vacation / weeks
They have been on vacation for weeks.
2 You / be on my game console / hours!
3 He / not watch TV / last weekend
4 We / stay in the same hotel / the last two weeks
5 I / not write my travel blog / a long time
6 We / eat local food / we arrived
7 They / not see their friends / Friday

4 **Complete the text about an unusual vacation. Use the verbs and choose *for* or *since*.**

Jill Daniels [1] *has had* (have) a new bike [2] *for / since* Christmas. When she got her bike, she went on a biking trip. She [3] .... (be) on her trip [4] *for / since* three months now, and she [5] .... (travel) thousands of kilometers. She [6] .... (visit) six different countries, and she [7] .... (be) in Portugal [8] *for / since* Thursday. However, she [9] .... (not stay) in a hotel or put up a tent [10] *for / since* December. Why? Because Jill's bike [11] .... (not leave) her house! "It's a virtual vacation on an exercise bike," explains Jill. "I bike 20 kilometers every day. I haven't gotten a tan, and I [12] .... (not buy) any souvenirs, but I'm enjoying it!"

5 **Make questions and answers about Exercise 4.**

1 How long / Jill / had a new bike?
How long has Jill had a new bike? Since Christmas.
2 How long / she / be on her trip?
3 How long / she / be in Portugal?
4 How many kilometers / she / travel?
5 How many countries / she visit?

Pronunciation /aɪ/ vs /ɪ/

6a 2.17 **Listen and repeat.**

active	arrive	bike	give	I've	like
live	sign	miss	since	time	visit

b **Copy the table and put the words in Exercise 6a in the correct column.**

/aɪ/	/ɪ/
arrive	*active*

c 2.18 **Listen, check and repeat.**

7 **What about you? In pairs, ask and answer.**

1 How long have you lived in your town/city?
2 How long have you had a cell phone?
3 How long have you known your best friend?

How long have you lived in your town?

I've lived here for ten years.

Vocabulary • Meanings of *get*

1 Match the pictures (1–6) to the different meanings of the verb *get* (a–f).

a It was dark when we got to the campsite. = arrive
b Damian got a key ring and a baseball cap from the souvenir shop. = buy *1*
c We got their postcard after they arrived home from their vacation. = receive
d Can you get the bottle of sunscreen from our hotel room? = bring
e It was getting cold on the beach, so we went home. = become
f He got on the bus and bought a ticket. = walk/move

Word list page 27
Workbook page 128

2 Read the sentences. Replace *get* with one of these verbs in the correct form.

~~arrive~~ become buy bring receive walk

1 Hurry up! We won't get to school on time!
Hurry up! We won't arrive at school on time!
2 I think adventure vacations are getting more dangerous.
3 When you book a flight online, you get the tickets in an email.
4 She got a lot of new clothes for her vacation.
5 Can you get the guidebook? I left it in my bag.
6 Someone checked our passports before we got onto the plane.

3 What would you say in these situations? Make a question or a sentence with *get*.

1 You like your friend's new bag. You want to know where she bought it.
Where did you get your bag?
2 You sent your friend a text message. You want to know if he received it.
Did you .... ?
3 You see your friends at a party. You ask them what time they arrived.
When .... ?
4 You are at a train station with a friend. Your train has arrived.
Come on. Let's .... .
5 Your mother has left her jacket upstairs. You offer to bring it to her.
Don't worry. I'll .... .

4 What about you? In pairs, ask and answer.

1 How many text messages do you get a day?
2 What time do you usually get to school?
3 What things can you do to get healthy?
4 How often do you get on a bus to go to school?

How many text messages do you get a day?

I get about twenty text messages a day.

Brain Trainer Unit 5 Activity 3
Go to page 63

Chatroom Asking for information

Speaking and Listening

1 Look at the photo. Answer the questions.

1 Where do you think they have been?
2 What are they doing?
3 What do you think Tom's dad is asking?

2 Listen and read the conversation.
2.19 **Check your answers.**

3 Listen and read again. Answer the questions.
2.19
1 Who liked the souvenir shops? *Tom*
2 What does Ash want to do?
3 Where does Tom want to go next?
4 How does the girl help them?
5 How can they get there?
6 What does Ash want to know?

4 Act out the conversation in groups of four.

Mr. Green	What did you think of Brighton Pier, boys?
Tom	I really liked the souvenir shops.
Ash	The cafés were nice, too. Can we have lunch soon?
Tom	You just had ice cream, Ash! Let's go see Brighton Pavilion first.
Ash	Is it far?
Mr. Green	Let's ask someone. Excuse me. Can you help us? We want to get to Brighton Pavilion.
Girl	Sure. Let me show you on the map. You're here … and Brighton Pavilion is there. You can't miss it.
Mr. Green	How can we get there?
Girl	Well, you just missed the bus, but it's only a ten-minute walk.
Ash	Is there a good place to eat there?
Girl	Oh yes! There's a really good restaurant there. The menu just changed, and the food's delicious.
Ash	Thank goodness. I'm starving!

Say it in your language …
Thank goodness.
I'm starving!

5 **Look back at the conversation. Who says what?**

1 Is it far? *Ash*
2 Excuse me. Can you help us?
3 How can we get there?
4 Is there a good place to eat there?

6 **Read the phrases for asking for information.**

Asking for information

Excuse me. Can you help us/me?
Where's a good place to …?
Is there a good place to … there?
How can we/I get there?
Is it far?
How long does it take to get to …?

7 2.20 **Listen to the conversations. What information do the people ask for? Act out the conversations in pairs.**

Ash	Excuse me. Can you help us? Where's a good place to [1] eat out?
Girl	There's a [2] pizza place near the beach.
Ash	Thanks. That's great.
Tom	Excuse me. Can you help me?
Girl	Sure.
Tom	Where's a good place to [1] buy souvenirs?
Girl	There's a [2] great shop in the Brighton Pavilion.
Tom	Is it far?
Girl	[3] No. It's only a five-minute walk.

8 **Work in pairs. Replace the words in purple in Exercise 7. Use these words and/or your own ideas. Act out the conversations.**

Excuse me. Can you help us? Where's a good place to buy a map?

There's a newsstand near the station.

1 buy clothes / have a drink / go swimming

2 good store in the mall / café near the pier / swimming pool near the park

3 No. It's about five minutes by bus. / Yes. It's about a twenty-minute walk. / No. It's right there.

Grammar • Past simple with *just*

You just had ice cream.
You just missed the bus.
The menu just changed.

Grammar reference page 118

1 **Study the grammar table. Choose the correct option to complete the rule.**

The Past simple with *just* describes an action that happened *a short time ago / a long time ago*.

2 **Make sentences with *just*.**

1 He / get a hamburger and fries
He just got a hamburger and fries.
2 I / get a postcard from my friend
3 She / go for a swim
4 We / pack our bags
5 He / buy some souvenirs
6 I / find the guidebook
7 They / check into their hotel

3 **In pairs, say what just happened. Use the ideas below.**

book a hotel	his brother/tell a joke
leave the house	lose their luggage
put up a tent	start their homework
their team/win a game	

1 He's excited.
2 They're worried.
3 We're tired.
4 He's laughing.
5 She isn't home.
6 They're happy.
7 You're bored.

Why is he excited?

He just booked a hotel.

Reading

1 **Look at the photos of these tourist attractions. Which would you like to visit? Why?**

Strange Tourist Attractions

This week in *Vacation Vistas* you can read about tourist attractions with a difference.

Bubble Gum Alley, San Luis Obispo, California, US

In 1950, this was just a normal passage between buildings. Then students from two local schools started to leave their bubble gum on its walls. They wrote messages with the gum and made pictures. Some people loved the bubble gum in the alley, but others hated it, and local store owners cleaned it a few times. But the students and their bubble gum always came back.

Today the alley is called Bubble Gum Alley, and it is still full of gum. Students leave most of it, but tourists and artists leave gum, too. Artist Matthew Hoffman recently made a big picture of a man blowing a bubble! "It's fantastic!" says one visitor. "Disgusting!" says another. What do *you* think?

Upside Down House, Szymbark, Poland

Daniel Czapiewski built this house in 2007, and thousands of tourists have visited it since then. He built it because he thinks many things in the world are wrong—upside down—and his house is a symbol of this.

You usually enter a house through the door, but to get into the Upside Down House, you climb through a window. When you are inside, you walk along the ceiling, go under a table and look up at a bed. In the bathroom, there's a toilet on the ceiling; in the living room there's an upside down TV.

Inside the house, there's an art exhibition. It's called "Let's Save This World," and the pictures show different world problems. Czapiewski wants people to think about these things. "I just visited the house, and I like its message," said one tourist, "but it made me feel dizzy!"

Key Words

tourist attractions	passage
bubble gum	blowing a bubble
upside down	dizzy

2 (2.21) **Read the magazine article. Match the statements to the attractions. (A = Bubble Gum Alley, B = Upside Down House)**

1 Some people don't like it. *A*
2 Furniture is in the wrong place.
3 It's popular with students.
4 It has something important to say.
5 You can walk along it.
6 You feel confused inside.
7 You can see serious pictures there.
8 You can see a funny picture there.

3 **Read the article again. Are the statements true (T) or false (F)?**

1 The first people to leave bubble gum in the alley were artists. *F*
2 Some people tried to clean the walls in the alley.
3 Everybody loves Bubble Gum Alley.
4 The Upside Down House represents what the artist thinks is wrong with the world.
5 You go into the house through a window.
6 The TV is in the living room.

Listening

1 (2.22) **Listen to the radio interview. Then complete the sentence.**

The most unusual place Troy has ever stayed in is in .... .

Listening Bank Unit 5 page 66

2 **Think about a tourist attraction in your country.**

1 Where is it?
2 What is it?
3 What is it like? Describe it.
4 How long has it been a tourist attraction?
5 Who visits the place and why? What do people think of it?

Writing • A travel guide

1 Read the Writing File.

Writing File Making your writing more interesting

- Use different adjectives to make your writing more interesting.
- Use new vocabulary you have learned, too. It's a good way to remember new words!

2 Read the travel guide. Find the opposites of these adjectives.

1 large *small*
2 unfriendly
3 rainy
4 ugly
5 unknown
6 terrible

Travel Guide

Brighton

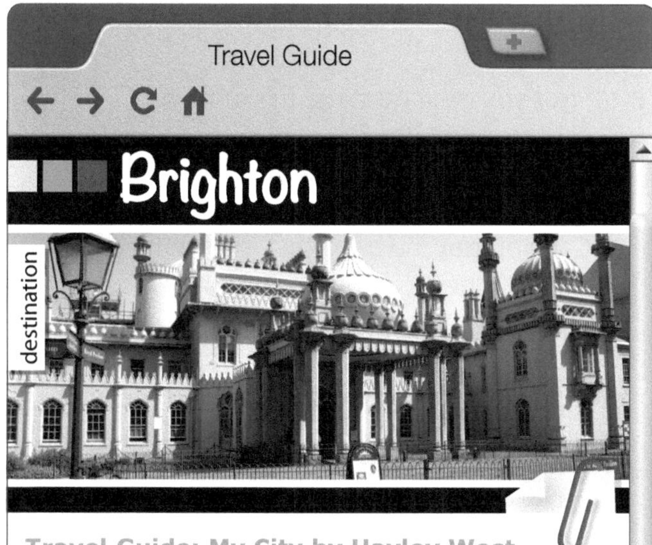

Travel Guide: My City by Hayley West

My hometown is Brighton. It's a small city, near the sea, in southern England. I love living in Brighton because the people are friendly, and the weather is usually sunny. There are also a lot of music festivals here.

There are many things to see and do in Brighton. One of the main attractions is Brighton Pavilion. It's a beautiful palace, and it's more than two hundred years old! Another famous attraction is Brighton Pier. There's a fantastic amusement park there. You can also sit in a beach café or buy some souvenirs. If you enjoy watersports, you can go windsurfing or sailing, too.

Brighton is a great city and has a lot to offer. When you visit Brighton, get a newspaper and see what's going on. You might get a nice surprise!

3 Find the adjectives in these sentences. Then copy and complete the table.

1 San Francisco is a big city, and it's very busy.
2 The most popular attraction is the Golden Gate Bridge.
3 There's an interesting museum and a famous park, too.
4 People are usually helpful and friendly.
5 The weather is often foggy and cold.

Town/City	*big, busy*
People	
Weather	
Tourist attractions	

4 Read the travel guide again. Answer the questions.

1 Where is Brighton? *It's in southern England.*
2 What are the people like there?
3 What is the weather like?
4 What are the main attractions?
5 How can you find out what's happening in Brighton?

5 Think about your town or city. Answer the questions. Take notes.

1 Where is it?
2 What do you think of it?
3 What are the people like?
4 Is the weather usually good or bad?
5 Are there any famous tourist attractions?
6 What activities can you do there?

6 Write a travel guide. Use "My favorite town/city" and your notes from Exercise 5.

My favorite town/city 

1 Introduce your town/city.
2 Describe what you can see and do.
3 Give your conclusion.

Remember!

- Use different adjectives to make your writing more interesting.
- Use the vocabulary in this unit.
- Check your grammar, spelling and punctuation.

Refresh Your Memory!

Grammar • Review

1 Match the beginnings (1–8) to the endings (a–h) of the sentences.

1 They've been on vacation for *b*
2 He's lived in southern California since
3 I waited two hours for
4 She hasn't written her travel blog for
5 I haven't worn a T-shirt since
6 We've tried a lot of different sports since
7 They haven't had a sunny day for
8 I haven't received a text message since

a a long time. She has a lot to write about.
b three weeks. They don't want to go home.
c he was a child. He speaks fluent Spanish.
d weeks. It's been very cloudy.
e last weekend. I miss my friends!
f we arrived. We've been really busy!
g a train this morning. I was fed up.
h Monday. It's been too cold!

2 Complete the sentences. Use *just* and these verbs.

arrive	buy	eat	~~finish~~
get	have	miss	pass

1 Sorry, there isn't any more pizza. We *just finished* it.
2 They .... some souvenirs. They don't have any more money.
3 That was the mail carrier. I .... a letter.
4 He's very tired. He .... home.
5 She's upset. She .... an argument with her mother.
6 I .... my exam. I'm very happy!
7 We .... the last bus. We'll have to walk home.
8 I .... the last slice of bread. I'll have to go to the supermarket later.

Vocabulary • Review

3 Complete the sentences with these verbs.

buy get packed ~~put up~~ stay went write

1 We arrived at the campsite, *put up* our tent, then made a pot of coffee.
2 Have you .... your bag? Yes, I'm ready to go.
3 I sometimes .... a travel blog on vacation.
4 If we take a map with us, we won't .... lost.
5 He doesn't .... souvenirs on vacation because he never has enough money.
6 We usually .... in a five-star hotel, but this year we .... camping.

4 Match the meanings of *get* (a–f) to the sentences (1–6).

a arrive *2*
b buy
c receive
d bring
e become
f walk/move

1 I **got** your text message this morning. What's the matter?
2 I was late for school this morning. I **got** there at nine thirty!
3 Can you **get** the basketball? It's in the car.
4 He **got** a new computer game with his birthday money.
5 School exams **are getting** more difficult.
6 When the school bus arrived, we all **got** on.

Speaking • Review

5 2.23 **Put the conversation in the correct order. Then listen and check.**

a No. It's only a five-minute walk.
b Excuse me. Can you help me? *1*
c There's a good souvenir shop on Cedar Street.
d Where's a good place to buy postcards?
e Sure.
f Is it far?

Dictation

6 2.24 **Listen and write in your notebook.**

My assessment profile: page 141

Gulliver's Travels

by Jonathan Swift

Introduction

It's 1726 and Gulliver is traveling across the ocean from England. There's a storm, and his boat is shipwrecked. He arrives in a strange country called Lilliput. He meets very small people there. Later he travels to other countries and meets very big people and horses. They all ask Gulliver about his country and how it is different. Are people better or worse there? Gulliver returns home, but his adventures change his ideas and his life.

Chapter 1—I came to Lilliput

I woke up after nine hours. It was daylight and I was on my back. I tried to stand up, but I could not move! I turned my head a little and looked around me. I saw thousands of strings across my body.

... Then something moved on my foot. It moved over my body and up to my face. I looked down and saw a man. He was smaller than my hand. Forty more little men followed him ... The man began to speak. His words were strange to me, but I watched his hands. "We will not hurt you," I understood. "But do not try and run away, or we will kill you." I put up my hand and showed him: "I will stay here." Then I had an idea. I also put my hand to my mouth: "I am hungry." The man understood me. He shouted to the people on the ground. A hundred men climbed onto my body and walked up to my mouth. They carried food for me. It came from the king, they told me later.

Reading

1 Look at the picture of Gulliver from the book *Gulliver's Travels*. Answer the questions.

1 Where is he?
2 What is happening?
3 How do you think the little people feel?

2 Read the Introduction and the extract from Chapter 1. Were your predictions correct?

3 Read the Introduction again. Choose the correct options. 2.25

1 Gulliver goes to Lilliput *on vacation* / *by accident*.
2 He meets *very big* / *very small* people there.
3 He meets horses *in the same place* / *in another country*.
4 After his adventures, Gulliver *changes* / *doesn't change* his life.

Gulliver's boat is shipwrecked.

4 Read the extract from Chapter 1. Answer the questions. 2.26

1 What happened when Gulliver woke up?
He couldn't move because he was tied up.
2 How are the Lilliputians different from Gulliver?
3 How many men were on Gulliver?
4 How does Gulliver talk to the little man?
5 How do the people help him?
6 What type of ruler does Lilliput have?

My Literature File

5 Take notes about a book you have read. It can be about a journey or an experience of a strange new place. Think about:

- when and where the story happens
- who is/are the main character(s)
- new places he/she goes (they go) to
- new people he/she meets (they meet)
- what happens in the end

6 Write an Introduction to the book. Add photos or pictures. Use your notes from Exercise 5 to help you.

6 That's Life!

Grammar
Have to, don't have to, must, mustn't; Predictions with *will, won't, might*

Vocabulary
Household chores; Feelings adjectives

Speaking
Giving advice (*should, shouldn't*)

Writing
A problem page

Word list page 27
Workbook page 129

Vocabulary • Household chores

1 2.27 **Match the pictures (1–16) to these phrases. Then listen, check and repeat.**

clear the table	cook a meal	do the dishes	do the ironing
do the laundry	feed the cat	hang out the laundry	load the dishwasher
make your bed *1*	mow the lawn	set the table	sweep the floor
take out the trash	vacuum the floor	walk the dog	wash the car

2 **Complete the sentences with the household chores from Exercise 1.**

1 First, *cook a meal* and *set the table*. Then you can eat.
2 .... with all the dirty plates or, if you don't have a dishwasher, ... after the meal.
3 If there are pieces of food under the table, ... or .... .
4 When you have dirty clothes, ... , and then .... to dry.
5 If your clothes are wrinkled, ...
6 When the trash can in the kitchen is full, ...
7 .... every day. Pets can't live without food.
8 When the grass is too high, ...
9 .... every day. Dogs need a lot of exercise.
10 .... on the driveway so it looks nice and clean.

3 **In pairs, ask and answer.**

1 What chores do you do at mealtimes?
I always set and clear the table, and I sometimes cook dinner on Saturdays.
2 What chores do other people in your family do?
3 What other chores do you do in the house?

Brain Trainer Unit 6 Activity 2
Go to page 63

Reading

Read the webpage quickly. Choose the best title.

1 The World's Laziest Teenager
2 Teens Work Harder Than Their Parents
3 Today's Teens Don't Do Chores

2 2.28 **Read the webpage again. Are these statements true (T) or false (F)?**

1 Cleaning the bathroom is a more popular chore with teenagers than doing the ironing. *F*
2 More than half of all teenagers have never cooked a meal.
3 Dr. Sheila Green thinks teenagers are lazy.
4 She thinks teenagers will be good at their jobs.
5 Dan Sparks thinks that many teenagers do a lot of homework.
6 He thinks it's more important that teenagers do homework, sports and music than chores.
7 Linda Fiorelli makes her children do chores.
8 Linda Fiorelli thinks children don't learn anything when they do chores.

What about you? **In pairs, ask and answer.**

1 How much free time do you have every day?
2 How much time do you spend on household chores?
3 Do you think you do a fair share of the household chores? Why?/Why not?

How much free time do you have every day?

Not much—I do a lot of sports after school.

I have a lot of free time—about two or three hours, I think.

TeenWorld.com

A study of American teenagers has found that most of them have never done any household chores. Many young people aged 11 to 16 don't have to make their bed. Thirty-five percent have never cooked a meal, sixty-three percent have never done the ironing, and more than seventy-five percent have never done the laundry or cleaned the bathroom.

Dr. Sheila Green is one of the authors of the study. "This information is very worrying," she says. "Every year, teenagers are getting lazier. Real jobs in the real world will be very difficult for them."

Dan Sparks, from the parents' website FamilyFirst.com, disagrees. "Young people today work very hard—harder than their parents, sometimes. Many of them have to do three hours of homework every night. Playing on a sports team or learning a musical instrument can take a lot of time too, and these activities are an important part of teenagers' lives. If we want young people with good test scores and also some interests outside school, we shouldn't give them chores."

Linda Fiorelli, author of *The Happy Home*, feels very differently. "It's about respect, not time. Even my five-year-old son has to set the table every day. It takes one minute, but it's important. Children share the house with their parents, so they must share the jobs around the house, too. That's fair, and it teaches good habits for the future."

Grammar • Have to/Don't have to

Affirmative
I/You/We/They have to set the table. He/She/It has to set the table.

Negative
I/You/We/They don't have to set the table. He/She/It doesn't have to set the table.

Questions
Do you have to do any chores? Yes, I do./No, I don't. Does he have to do any chores? Yes, he does./No, he doesn't.

Grammar reference page 120

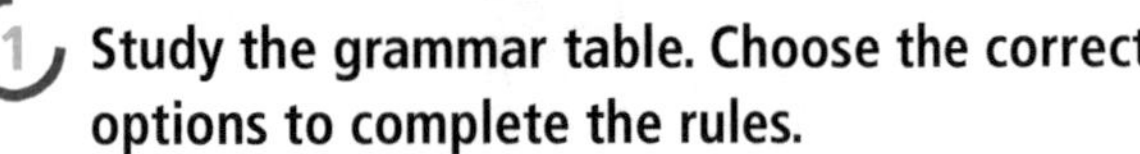

1 Study the grammar table. Choose the correct options to complete the rules.

1 We use *have to* when something *is / isn't* necessary.
2 We use *don't have to* when something *is / isn't* necessary.

2 Find more examples in the article on page 15.

3 Make sentences and questions.

1 clear / the table / has / She / to
She has to clear the table.
2 the dog / don't / to / We / have / walk
3 I / Do / do / have / any chores / to / ?
4 doesn't / vacuum / the floor / He / to / have
5 They / the laundry / to / hang out / have
6 go / Why / you / have / to / do / ?

4 Complete the sentences. Use the verbs and the form of *have to.*

1 We *have to clean up* (clean up) our bedroom every week.
2 My parents .... (not cook) dinner tonight. We're going to a restaurant.
3 He .... (help) me! I can't do it on my own.
4 I'm really dirty! I .... (take) a shower before I go out.
5 .... (they/do) any homework tonight?
6 My sister .... (not make) her bed in the morning because she's only three.

5 Make questions with *have to.*

1 Clara and David / cook dinner?
Do Clara and David have to cook dinner?
2 Mom / clean the living room?
3 Dad / feed the cat?
4 Clara and David / load the dishwasher?
5 Clara / wash the car?
6 David / clean up his bedroom?

6 Look at the note. Answer the questions in Exercise 5.

1 *No, they don't. Dad has to cook dinner.*

Chores for today

cook dinner	Dad
clean the living room	Mom
feed the cat	David
load the dishwasher	Clara and David
wash the car	Dad
clean up his bedroom	David

• Must/Mustn't

Obligation
I must leave now. It's late. I have to help my mom.

No obligation
I don't have to cook any meals.

Prohibition
You mustn't talk in the library.

Grammar reference page 120

7 Study the grammar table. Do these words mean the same thing?

1 *must* and *have to*
2 *mustn't* and *don't have to*

8 Replace the words in bold in each sentence so they have the same meaning. Use these words.

I don't have to | I have to | ~~I must~~ | I mustn't

1 **I have to** take out the trash. *I must take out the trash.*
2 **It isn't necessary to** mow the lawn.
3 **I must** do a lot of chores.
4 **I can't** swim here.

9 Choose the correct options.

I'm on a swimming team, and it's hard work. We [1] *must / don't have to* swim for an hour before school. I [2] *mustn't / have to* get up at 6 a.m. because school starts at 8:30, and we [3] *mustn't / don't have to* be late for class! We [4] *mustn't / have to* practice every morning from Monday to Friday. On Saturdays there are swim meets, and we [5] *must / don't have to* be fast if we want to stay on the team. On Sundays there are no meets, so we [6] *mustn't / don't have to* go to the swimming pool. I love Sundays!

10 Make true sentences about your country. Use the correct form of *must, mustn't, have to* or *don't have to*.

1 When you're a baby, you .... go to school.
2 Students .... be polite to their teachers.
3 You .... use your cell phone in class.
4 We .... wear a school uniform.
5 You .... throw trash in the street.

Pronunciation /ʌ/ and /yu/

11a Listen and repeat. Think about the pronunciation of the underlined *u*. 2.29

bus | confused | museum
under | upset | usually

b Listen and repeat. Then practice saying the sentences. 2.30

1 We don't use gloves in summer.
2 Some of us saw a funny sculpture at the museum.
3 Tuesday was a beautiful, sunny summer's day.
4 My mom made some tuna for lunch.

Vocabulary • Feelings adjectives

1 Look at these words. Check the meaning in a dictionary. Listen and repeat. 2.31

confident | confused | disappointed
embarrassed | fed up | glad | grateful
guilty | jealous | lonely | nervous
relaxed | relieved | upset

Word list page 27
Workbook page 129

2 Match the sentences to the words from Exercise 1.

1 I was really worried, but now everything's OK. *relieved*
2 It's not fair! Why can't I have that?
3 I was hoping for a better result.
4 Thank you so much!
5 My exam starts in a minute. Help me!
6 My exam starts in a minute. I think I can do well on it.
7 No one ever talks to me.
8 I'm so sorry that I hurt your feelings.

3 Read the short texts. How do the people feel? Make sentences using these words.

confused | embarrassed | ~~fed up~~
glad | guilty | jealous
~~nervous~~ | relaxed | upset

1 It's Sam's first day at a new school. He's been to three different schools in the last three years. *Sam is nervous, and he's fed up because he has to change schools so often.*
2 Ginny thinks she sees her friend in the street. She runs up to him and says hello. But this person is Connor, and he's never met Ginny before.
3 Jack loves Emily, and Emily loves Jack, but Sophie loves Jack, too. She cries when she sees him. Jack wants Sophie to be happy.
4 Ben doesn't have to do anything today, so he's lying in the sun. It's a beautiful day.

Brain Trainer Unit 6 Activity 3
Go to page 63

Chatroom Giving advice

Speaking and Listening

1 **Look at the photo. Answer the questions.**

1 Who has a problem?
2 What do you think it is?

2 **Listen and read the conversation.**
2.32 **Check your answers.**

3 **Listen and read again. Choose the correct options.**
2.32
1 Ruby *is / isn't* happy.
2 She *has / hasn't* finished her homework.
3 She usually does her homework *on the weekend / on school nights*.
4 She *has to / doesn't have to* do chores on school nights.
5 *Ruby / Ruby's parents* usually walk(s) the dog.
6 Ruby *goes / doesn't go* to climbing club.

4 **Act out the conversation in groups of three.**

Tom What's wrong, Ruby? You look kind of fed up.
Ruby I am. I've done six hours of homework today!
Tom Maybe you should take a rest.
Ruby A rest? I wish! I haven't even started my math, and that'll be really hard …
Ella You won't have any problems with it, I'm sure. You're great at math! But maybe you shouldn't do all your homework on the weekend, Ruby.
Ruby I don't have enough time for homework on school nights.
Ella Why don't you talk to your parents about your chores? Maybe *they* can walk the dog in the evening, and you can study.
Ruby No, they're too busy. I might stop going to climbing club so I have more time.
Tom I don't think you should stop climbing, Ruby. You love it!

Say it in your language …
What's wrong?
I wish!

5 Look back at the conversation. Complete these sentences.

1 Maybe you *should* take a rest.
2 Maybe you .... do all your homework on the weekend.
3 Why .... you talk to your parents?
4 I don't .... you should stop climbing.

6 Read the phrases for giving advice.

Positive	Negative
Maybe you should …	Maybe you shouldn't …
I think you should …	I don't think you should …
Why don't you …?	

7 Listen to the conversation. What two pieces of advice does Tom give Ella? Act out the conversation in pairs.
2.33

Ella I can't [1] find my school sweater!
Tom Why don't you [2] clean up your room?
Ella No, I can't do that. [3] I don't have time now. I know! I can [4] wear your sweater.
Tom I don't think you should do that. [5] It's too big. Maybe you should [6] borrow a sweater from Ruby.

8 Work in pairs. Replace the words in purple in Exercise 7. Use these words and/or your own ideas. Act out the conversations.

I can't find my
cell phone!

Why don't you look in the living room?

1 do my homework / find a birthday present for Mom / sleep at night

2 ask your sister for help / buy that bag / read a book in bed

3 She never helps. / I can't afford it. / I hate reading.

4 skip school / give her a pen / buy a new bed

5 You're too lazy. / It's too boring. / It's too expensive.

6 work harder / look for something at the market / drink hot chocolate before bed

Grammar • Predictions with *will*, *won't*, *might*

Definite
I think she'll be relieved.
You won't have any problem, I'm sure.
Will they finish it?

Possible
I might see them tomorrow. I'm not sure.
He might not like the movie.

Watch Out!
will not = won't
might not = ~~mightn't~~

Grammar reference page 120

1 Study the grammar table. Complete the rules with *will* or *might*.

1 We use .... when we are sure about something in the future.
2 We use .... when we aren't sure about something in the future.
3 The contracted form of .... is *'ll*.
4 The contracted form of .... is *won't*.

2 Choose the correct options in Ruby's predictions.

1 Ella and Tom *will* / *might* go to the movies with me. They haven't decided.
2 Ash *won't* / *might not* like the movie. He hates romantic comedies.
3 Bad weather *won't* / *might not* be a problem at an indoor swimming pool.
4 I'm sure the math test *will* / *might* be difficult.
5 I *won't* / *might not* pass the test. I'm not sure.

3 Complete the predictions. Use *will* or *might* and contracted forms where possible.

1 One day I*'ll be* (be) famous. I know it!
2 My team .... (win) the game. We're pretty good, but the other team is pretty good, too.
3 I .... (not finish) my English homework tonight. I'm not sure.
4 They think he .... (arrive) after lunch.
5 .... (you/have) time to wash the car?

Reading

1 **Look at the picture of a teenager of the future. How is his life different from the lives of teenagers today?**

What kind of life will teenagers have fifty years from now? No one can be sure, but experts have made some interesting predictions.

1 The home

Robots will make the beds, sweep the floor and do the laundry, so teenagers won't have to do many chores. Parents and teenagers might have a more relaxed relationship because of this. Or will they just find other things to argue about?

2 School

Some people might travel to school, but most people will study on their home computers and have virtual classes with the world's best teachers. One teacher might have a million students! All the classes will be in English, and everyone around the world will take the same exams.

3 Free time

Teenagers won't go to cafés and movie theaters with friends, but they won't be lonely. They'll have fun in a virtual world and go to amazing virtual parties with their favorite stars.

4 Entertainment

The movies of today will seem very boring because you can't change the story as you watch. In fifty years, all entertainment will be interactive—there will be no difference between video games and movies.

5 Fashion

Teenagers will be fatter than today because they won't do much exercise, so the most popular clothes will be very big and baggy. Global warming will bring changes in fashion, too. There will be air conditioning inside a lot of clothes—a big help in the hot temperatures around the world.

In fifty years, you will be old and gray. What will you think of the teens of the future?

Key Words

relationship	argue
virtual	baggy
global warming	air conditioning

2 **Read the magazine article and check your answer to Exercise 1.**

3 2.34 **Read these headings. Which paragraph do you think will mention these things? Read the article quickly to check.**

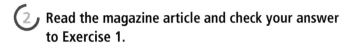

clothes *5*	chores	exams	languages
parents	parties	video games	

4 2.34 **Read the article again. Answer the questions.**

1 Why might parents and their teenage children have a better relationship in the future?
Because robots will do the teenagers' chores.
2 How will classes in the future be different from classes today? Find three differences.
3 Will teenagers enjoy their free time?
4 What will their parties be like?
5 What will future teenagers think of our movies?
6 Why will there be changes in fashion?

5 **Which predictions in the article do you think are**

1 correct? 2 silly? 3 exciting? 4 scary?

"There will be no difference between video games and movies." I think that's correct because it's starting to happen now.

Listening

1 2.35 **Listen to some teenagers of the future. Match the conversations (1–4) to the topics (A–D).**

A home
B school
C free time
D fashion

Listening Bank Unit 6 page 66

Writing • A problem page

1 **Read the Writing File.**

Writing File Linking words: reason and result

- **You can introduce a reason with *because*.**
  I feel guilty because I broke my dad's cell phone.
- **You can introduce a result with *so*.**
  I broke my dad's cell phone, so he's really angry with me.

2 **Read the problem page from a magazine. Find the linking words of reason and result.**

Problem Page

My mom works in a restaurant on Saturday nights, so I have to babysit my six-year-old sister. All my friends have fun together then, but I can't be with them. It isn't fair! What should I do?

Lateesha

I'm sure your mom is very grateful for your help on Saturdays, but you should talk to her about your problem. Choose a time when she isn't busy because it'll be easier to think of an answer to the problem then.

For example, someone else might be happy to babysit your sister some weeks. Other weeks, invite some friends to your house. You'll have more fun at home with your friends there. Cook them some nice food and watch a movie together. But remember, you mustn't make a lot of noise because your sister has to sleep. And clean up the house when they've left so your mom doesn't have to do any chores after a long evening at work.

You and your mom might have a lot of other good ideas, too. Good luck!

3 **Complete the sentences with *because* or *so*.**

1 I'm tired *because* I went to bed late last night.
2 He's jealous of his sister .... she's better at sports than him.
3 You've finished your homework, ... now you can watch a DVD.
4 I didn't do well in the race, ... I'm a little sad.
5 She's really upset .... her best friend yelled at her.

4 **Read the problem page again. Answer the questions.**

1 Who should Lateesha talk to about her problem? When?
She should talk to her mom when she isn't busy.
2 What idea does the writer have so that Lateesha can go out with her friends?
3 What idea does the writer have so that Lateesha can have more fun at home?
4 What two pieces of advice does the writer give about the second idea?

5 **Read about James's problem. Answer the questions. Take notes.**

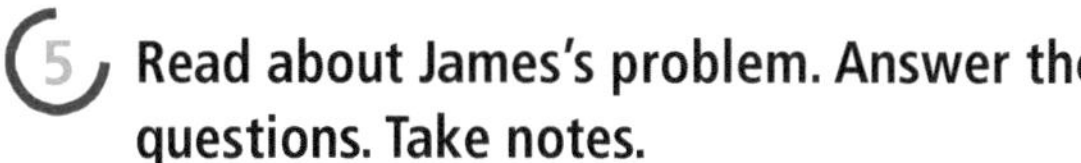

I moved to a new town last year. I have a lot of friends around the world because I play online games in my free time, but everyone at school is really unfriendly. I'm starting to feel pretty lonely. How can I make new friends here?

James

1 Is it normal to feel lonely in James's situation?
2 Should he talk to anyone about his problem?
3 Are school friends more important than online friends? Why?/Why not?
4 What can he do to make friends at school?
5 How do you think he'll feel after a few months?

6 **Write a letter giving advice to James. Use "My letter" and your notes from Exercise 5.**

My letter 

Paragraph 1
General advice for this problem
Paragraph 2
Specific ideas that might help
Paragraph 3
Encouraging ending

Remember!
- Use linking words for reason and result.
- Use the vocabulary in this unit.
- Check your grammar, spelling and punctuation.

Refresh Your Memory!

Grammar • Review

1 Make sentences and questions with *have to*.

1 we / learn English at school
We have to learn English at school.
2 you / study French?
3 my sister / not / do any homework
4 she / practice the piano every day
5 she / do any chores?
6 I / get up early for school
7 my parents / not / start work early

2 Complete the text with these words.

don't ~~have~~ has must mustn't to

My brother and I [1] *have* to stay with my grandparents this week. It's fun, but they have a lot of rules. For example, we [2] .... use our cell phones in the house because they hate cell phones. I [3] .... call my friends on the home phone. My brother [4] .... to walk the dog every day, but I [5] .... have to do that because I have a bad leg. I have [6] .... help Grandma with the cooking and ironing instead.

3 Complete the conversation. Use *will*, *won't* or *might* and the verbs.

A Do you want to come to the Smugglers concert on Saturday? I'm sure you [1] *will enjoy* (enjoy) it.
B I [2] .... (not be) here on Saturday, so I can't come with you.
A Where [3] .... (you/be)?
B In the mountains with my cousins.
A The weather forecast says it [4] .... (snow) in the mountains on the weekend. They're not sure.
B Cool! We [5] .... (go) snowboarding then, or we [6] .... (not do) anything. It's horrible outside when it's too cold and windy.

Vocabulary • Review

4 Match the beginnings (1–6) to the endings (a–f) of the sentences.

1 You should walk — b
2 She never does
3 Can you please mow
4 Remember to feed
5 I don't have to wash
6 We have to take out

a the cat.
b the dog.
c the ironing.
d the lawn?
e the trash.
f the car.

5 Complete the sentences with the correct feelings adjectives.

1 I like Mr. Green. I'm *glad* he's our teacher.
2 I'm really n _ _ _ _ _ _ about the concert. I might forget the words to all the songs!
3 I think someone stole my purse! Oh no, it's here. I'm so r _ _ _ _ _ _ _ !
4 You've really helped me. I'm so g _ _ _ _ _ _ _ .
5 I said some terrible things to her. I feel really g _ _ _ _ _ about that now.
6 I'm sure I can do it. I'm feeling very c _ _ _ _ _ _ _ _.

Speaking • Review

6 Complete the advice for these situations. Then listen and check. 2.36

1 **A** I'm late for school again!
B Why *don't you* get up earlier?
2 **A** I want to go to Antarctica on vacation.
B I .... you should do that. You hate cold weather!
3 **A** When I sweep the floor, it takes hours!
B Maybe .... vacuum the floor instead.
4 **A** I'm feeling pretty relaxed about the exams.
B I .... should be more worried. The exams are very important!
5 **A** When I load the dishwasher, I usually break a plate.
B Maybe .... do your chores so quickly.

Dictation

7 Listen and write in your notebook. 2.37

My assessment profile: page 142

Ben Powell's Profile

Age
19 years old

Home country
US

My favorite things …
theater, music, helping to prevent bullying

Reading

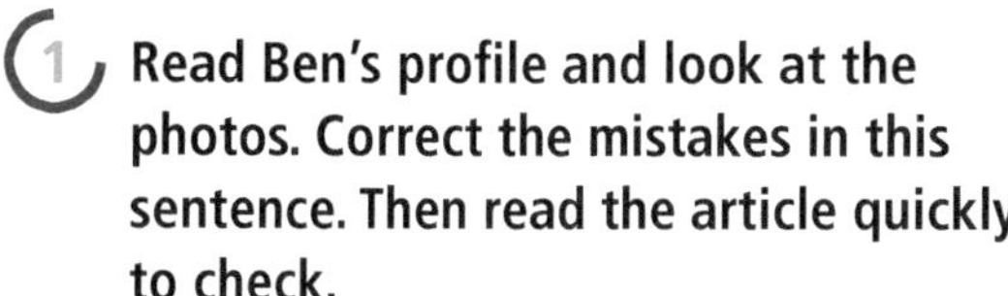

1 Read Ben's profile and look at the photos. Correct the mistakes in this sentence. Then read the article quickly to check.

Ben lives in Canada and has performed in a movie for people with bullying problems.

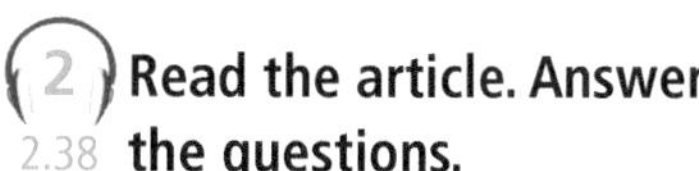

2 2.38 **Read the article. Answer the questions.**

1 What does Ben like to do?
He likes to play music and act.
2 Who worked with Ben on the play?
3 What did audience members see in the play?
4 What are some of the consequences of bullying?
5 What was the message of the play?

Ben's Story

Ben has enjoyed performing since he was three years old. Now nineteen, he is a musician (he plays the guitar and the trombone), a singer and an actor.

Ben and other students in his high school worked on a project with a very special message. Together with their drama teacher, they developed a play to present the consequences of bullying. They called it *Teen Reality*. Ben and his classmates helped with different parts of the dramatic production. They wrote the script, designed the set and acted in the play.

What was *Teen Reality* like? The audience walked through scenes showing a teen who is bullied, teenagers who bully others and those who witnessed the situation. The different scenes also presented the consequences of bullying, such as mental health issues and substance abuse. The students' production was a success. It became popular in their community, and it even appeared on a local television station.

Ben graduated from high school and started college, where he studies multimedia communications. He plans to join more organizations that work to prevent bullying. "My goal is to show people that there is no good excuse for bullying, no matter what the reason is," he says.

Key Words

play consequences bullying
script set

Class discussion

1 Are there problems with bullying in your country?
2 Are there any programs to help prevent bullying?
3 What can teenagers do to help prevent bullying?

Review 2

Grammar • Present perfect

1 Complete the sentences with the Present perfect form of the verbs.

1 *Have* you *ever been* (be) to Russia?
2 No. But I .... (always want) to go there.
3 I .... (never try) Japanese food.
4 Kelly .... (not finish) her project.
5 My brother .... (always want) to be a pilot.
6 The students .... (not do) their homework again.
7 Where .... you .... (be)? I .... (not see) you for a long time.

• Present perfect vs Past simple

2 Complete the conversations with the Present perfect or Past simple form of the verbs.

A [1] *Have* you *ever ridden* (ride) a camel?
B Yes, I [2] .... (ride) one. I [3] .... (take) a trip through the desert in Morocco once.
A When [4] .... you .... (go) to Morocco?
B We [5] .... (spend) a week there last year.

A When [6] .... you .... (come) back from vacation?
B I [7] .... (fly) back last night.
A What [8] .... (be) it like?
B Great! [9] .... you .... (ever go) to Florida?
A No, I [10] .... (not).

• Present perfect + *for* and *since*; *How long?*

3 Make sentences with *How long?* Complete the answers with *for* or *since*.

1 **A** you / live / in this house?
How long have you lived in this house?
2 **B** .... I was a child—so, ... fifteen years!
3 **A** your father / work / in the bank?
4 **B** .... five years.
5 **A** you have / the same hairstyle?
6 **B** .... I was about six!
7 **A** you know / your best friend?
8 **B** .... three years.
9 **A** your class / study / English?
10 **B** .... we were in elementary school.

• Past simple with *just*

4 Complete the sentences with *just* and the Past simple.

1 **A** Something smells delicious in your kitchen.
Did you just bake a cake? (bake)
2 **B** Yes! I .... it out of the oven. (take)
3 I'm really tired. I .... for a run around the park. (go)
4 Stella .... back from vacation. (arrive)
5 I .... my math homework—after two hours! (finish)
6 I'm crying, because I .... a sad movie on TV. (watch)

• Have to/Don't have to

5 Rewrite the sentences using the correct form of *have to* or *don't have to*.

1 It's essential to wear a helmet on a bike.
You have to wear a helmet.
2 It's not essential to book tickets in advance.
You .... tickets in advance.
3 Swimmers need swimming caps. It's a rule.
Swimmers .... wear swimming caps.
4 You can sit down if you are tired.
You .... stand.
5 You aren't allowed to arrive late.
You .... on time.
6 You can have lunch at school or at home. It's your choice.
You .... have lunch at school.

• Must/Mustn't

6 Make rules with *must* or *mustn't* for these signs.

1

You mustn't park here.

2

3

4

5

6

• Predictions with *will, won't, might*

7 Choose the correct option.

1 Look at those dark storm clouds. It *won't* / *will* rain later.
2 I'm not sure if I'm going to Mark's party. I *will* / *might* go.
3 They've been together for a really long time. I'm sure they *might* / *will* get married.
4 This answer *might* / *will* be right. I'm not sure.
5 I promise—I *might not* / *won't* tell anyone your secret.

Speaking • Doubt and disbelief

1 Complete the conversation with these words.

believe	impossible	~~kidding~~	Really

A Have you heard about this amazing coincidence? A man was walking under a window at the top of a building when a baby fell.
B You're [1] *kidding*!
A No, it's true. And he was passing at just the right time, so he caught the baby in his arms!
B No! [2] .... ?
A Yes, I read it in the paper. And then the same thing happened a few years later.
B I don't [3] .... it.
A It happened to the same man, outside the same building!
B That's [4] .... !
A I know, it's the strangest thing.

• Asking for information

2 Put the conversation in the correct order.

1 Excuse me, can you help me? I'm looking for the museum. Do you know where it is?
.... It's a nice walk from here, or you can take a bus.
.... Yes, I do. It's just across the river, on the left.
.... Oh yes, there are a lot of restaurants there.
.... I'd like to walk. But is it far?
.... OK, so we have to cross the river. How can we get to the river?
.... That doesn't sound too far. And are there any good places to eat near there?
.... No, it's about a twenty-minute walk.

• Giving advice

3 Complete the conversation with these phrases.

I don't think you should worry	Maybe you should tell
~~Why don't you talk~~	You shouldn't pretend

A What's wrong? You look really upset.
B I feel awful about my science exam results. I don't know how I'm going to tell my parents I did so badly. But I'm really bad at science, and I want to study drama instead.
A [1] *Why don't you talk* to your parents about it?
B The trouble is, they think I really like science.
A [2] .... them the truth.
B They'll be upset. After all, they're both doctors.
A [3] .... about that. They'll understand. [4] .... you're interested in something when you aren't.
B Yes, maybe you're right.

Vocabulary • News and media

1 Match the phrases (1–8) to their definitions (a–h).

1 an online diary *h*
2 the title of a newspaper article
3 a formal question-and-answer session with a person
4 a sudden news announcement
5 a person who writes newspaper articles
6 a newspaper article
7 a person who gives the news on TV
8 a news show that can be downloaded on an MP3 player

a interview
b journalist
c headline
d news flash
e news anchor
f podcast
g report
h blog

• Adverbs of manner

2 Complete the sentences with these adverbs.

angrily	carefully	early	fast
late	loudly	~~quietly~~	sadly

1 Please enter the room *quietly*—students are taking exams.
2 Can you speak more .... ? I can't hear you—it's very noisy in here.
3 Please drive ....—the roads are dangerous.
4 He's a fantastic athlete. He can run so .... .
5 "Go away," he said, quietly but .... .
6 I thought it would be a funny movie, but it ended so .... I cried.
7 If you don't get up soon, you'll arrive at school .... for your classes.
8 It's best to arrive ....—then we'll get the best seats in the theater.

• Vacation

3 Match the verbs (1–8) to the words (a–h) to make vacation phrases.

1 book
2 eat
3 go
4 pack
5 stay
6 get
7 put up
8 write

a a travel blog
b camping
c in a hotel
d a flight
e a tent
f a tan
g your bag
h out

• Meanings of *get*

4 Replace *get* using a different verb with the same meaning.

1 When my parents get old, I'll take care of them.
When my parents become old, I'll take care of them.
2 Can you get some milk when you go to the store?
3 What time will we get home?
4 Did you get an email from Laura about her party?
5 Get off the bus when you see a big gray building in front of you.
6 The dog ran very fast to get the ball.

• Household chores

5 Match the verbs (1–8) to the words (a–h) to make household chores.

1 clear
2 do
3 make
4 load
5 mow
6 sweep
7 take out
8 walk

a the floor
b your bed
c the dog
d the table
e the trash
f the lawn
g the ironing
h the dishwasher

• Feelings adjectives

6 Complete the sentences with these adjectives.

confident	confused	disappointed	glad
grateful	~~jealous~~	nervous	upset

1 Don't be *jealous* of people who seem to have more than you do.
2 My exam is tomorrow, but I'm not .... . I worked hard, so I'm .... I'll do well.
3 Could you explain that to me again? I'm .... .
4 Thank you very much. I'm very .... for your help.
5 Carla's .... because her cat died.
6 I'm so .... you're back! I missed you.
7 I'm .... that I didn't get the job.

Word list

Unit 4 • In the News

News and media

blog	/blɑg/
current affairs show	/ˌkʌrənt əˈfɛrz ʃoʊ/
headline	/ˈhɛdlaɪn/
international news	/ˌɪntəˈnæʃənəl ˈnuz/
interview (n, v)	/ˈɪntəˌvyu/
journalist	/ˈdʒənl-ɪst/
local news	/ˌloʊkəl ˈnuz/
national news	/ˌnæʃənl ˈnuz/
news anchor	/ˈnuz ˌæŋkə/
news flash	/ˈnuz flæʃ/
newspaper	/ˈnuzˌpeɪpə/
news website	/ˈnuz ˌwɛbsaɪt/
podcast	/ˈpɑdkæst/
report (n, v)	/rɪˈpɔrt/

Adverbs of manner

angrily	/ˈæŋgrəli/
badly	/ˈbædli/
carefully	/ˈkɛrfəli/
carelessly	/ˈkɛrlɪsli/
early	/ˈəli/
fast	/fæst/
happily	/ˈhæpəli/
hard	/hɑrd/
late	/leɪt/
loudly	/ˈlaʊdli/
patiently	/ˈpeɪʃəntli/
quietly	/ˈkwaɪətli/
sadly	/ˈsædli/
slowly	/ˈsloʊli/
well	/wɛl/

Unit 5 • Enjoy Your Vacation!

Vacation

book a flight	/ˌbʊk ə ˈflaɪt/
book a hotel	/ˌbʊk ə hoʊˈtɛl/
buy souvenirs	/ˌbaɪ ˌsuvəˈnɪr, ˈsuvəˌnɪr/
check into a hotel	/ˌtʃek ɪntʊ ə hoʊˈtɛl/
eat out	/ˌit ˈaʊt/
get a tan	/gɛt ə ˈtæn/
get lost	/gɛt ˈlɔst/
go camping	/ˌgoʊ ˈkæmpɪŋ/
go sightseeing	/ˌgoʊ ˈsaɪtˌsiɪŋ/
lose your luggage	/ˌluz yə ˈlʌgɪdʒ/
pack your bag	/ˌpæk yə ˈbæg/
put up a tent	/ˌpʊt ʌp ə tɛnt/
stay in a hotel	/ˌsteɪ ɪn ə həʊˈtel/
take a trip	/ˌteɪk ə ˈtrɪp/
write a travel blog	/ˌraɪt ə ˈtrævəl blɒg/

Meanings of *get*

arrive	/əˈraɪv/
become	/bɪˈkʌm/
bring	/brɪŋ/
buy	/baɪ/
move	/muːv/
receive	/rɪˈsiːv/
walk	/wɔːk/

Unit 6 • That's Life!

Household chores

clear the table	/ˌklɪr ðə ˈteɪbəl/
cook a meal	/ˌkʊk ə ˈmil/
do the dishes	/ˌdu ðə ˈdɪʃɪz/
do the ironing	/ˌdu ði ˈaɪənɪŋ/
do the laundry	/ˌdu ðə ˈlɔndri/
feed the cat	/ˌfid ðə ˈkæt/
hang out the laundry	/ˌhæŋ aʊt ðə ˈlɔndri/
load the dishwasher	/ˌloʊd ðə ˈdɪʃˌwɑʃə/
make your bed	/ˌmeɪk yə ˈbɛd/
mow the lawn	/ˌmoʊ ðə ˈlɔn/
set the table	/ˌsɛt ðə ˈteɪbəl/
sweep the floor	/ˌswip ðə ˈflɔr/
take out the trash	/ˌteɪk aʊt ðə ˈtræʃ/
vacuum the floor	/vækyum ðə ˈflɔr/
walk the dog	/ˌwɔk ðə ˈdɔg/
wash the car	/ˌwɑʃ ðə ˈkɑr/

Feelings adjectives

confident	/ˈkɑnfədənt/
confused	/kənˈfyuzd/
disappointed	/ˌdɪsəˈpɔɪntɪd/
embarrassed	/ɪmˈbærəst/
fed up	/ˌfɛd ˈʌp/
glad	/glæd/
grateful	/ˈgreɪtfəl/
guilty	/ˈgɪlti/
jealous	/ˈdʒɛləs/
lonely	/ˈloʊnli/
nervous	/ˈnəvəs/
relaxed	/rɪˈlækst/
relieved	/rɪˈlivd/
upset	/ˌʌpˈset/

Make a Difference

Grammar
Be going to and *will*;
First conditional

Vocabulary
Protest and support;
Verb + preposition

Speaking
Persuading

Writing
A formal letter

Word list page 61
Workbook page 130

Vocabulary • Protest and support

1 3.1 **Match the items in the photos (1–12) to these words. Then listen, check and repeat.**

banner
charity
collection
demonstration
donation
fundraising event
march *1*
petition
sign
sit-in
slogan
volunteer

2 **Complete the sentences with the words in Exercise 1.**

1 Students are having a *sit-in* at school today.
2 This T-shirt has an interesting .... on it.
3 Did you sign the .... against the new road?
4 A .... or sign always carries a strong message.
5 We're taking up a .... for a local charity.
6 They're hosting a dinner as a .... . They want to make a lot of money for the hospital.
7 There are a lot of .... for the fun run. We have a lot of help.

3 What about you? **In pairs, ask and answer.**

1 Have you ever made a donation to a charity? Which one?
2 Have you ever been a volunteer? Who for?
3 Do you have a T-shirt with a slogan on it? What does the slogan say?
4 Have there been any marches or sit-ins in your city or town? What were they for?

Have you ever made a donation to a charity?

Yes, I have. I've made donations to the World Wildlife Fund.

Brain Trainer Unit 7 Activity 2
Go to page 64

Reading

Look at the text and the photos. Answer the questions.

1 What type of text is it? An article, a letter, a pamphlet?
2 What do you think the topic is?

Read and check your answers to Exercise 1.

3.2 **Read the text again. Match the headings to paragraphs A–D.**

1 Why did this happen? *B*
2 What are Elephant Family's plans?
3 What's the problem?
4 How can you help?

Read the text again. Answer the questions.

1 Where do Asian elephants live?
In India, Thailand, Malaysia and Indonesia.
2 How many Asian elephants are there?
3 How do the elephants look for food?
4 Why do people kill the elephants?
5 What are "elephant corridors"?
6 What type of event is Elephant Parade?
7 How can you help the charity Elephant Family?

In pairs, ask and answer.

1 Do you think Elephant Parade is a good idea? Why?/Why not?
2 Have there been any outdoor art exhibitions in your city or town? Describe them.

Dana Point Elephant Parade

You don't usually see elephants in southern California, but you'll probably meet one near the beach this weekend! This summer there are going to be dozens of elephant sculptures around beaches, parks and resorts in Dana Point, California. They're part of an art exhibition called Elephant Parade. Elephant Parade works with the charity Elephant Family. With your help, we're going to save the Asian elephant.

A ....
Today there are only 25,000 Asian elephants in India, Thailand, Malaysia and Indonesia. A hundred years ago there were 200,000 elephants in these countries.

B ....
The elephants are competing with people for food and space. Asian elephants travel from forest to forest, looking for food. Today the forests are getting smaller, and the elephants go through villages to get to them. People in the villages protect their land and kill the elephants. In thirty years there won't be any elephants unless we do something.

C ....
The charity Elephant Family is going to make "elephant corridors." They're special roads between the forests where elephants can travel safely. There's already one in India, but we need many more.

D ....
Come and see Elephant Parade. The parade isn't a march, so we won't have banners or slogans. It's a fundraising event. After the exhibition we're going to sell the sculptures. You can buy smaller elephants or T-shirts at our website, or make a donation and sign our petition.
The future is in our hands. Help us save the Asian elephant.

Grammar • Be going to

Affirmative

There are going to be dozens of elephant sculptures.
The charity is going to make "elephant corridors."

Negative

There aren't going to be dozens of elephant sculptures.
The charity isn't going to make "elephant corridors."

Questions and short answers

Are they going to make them?
Yes, they are./No, they aren't.
What are they going to do?

Grammar reference page 122

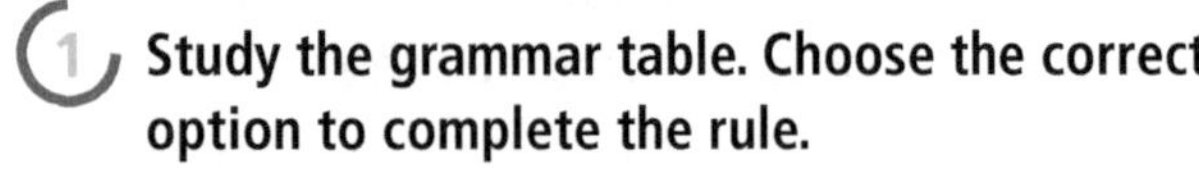

1 Study the grammar table. Choose the correct option to complete the rule.

1 We use **be going to** to talk about *the future / the present.*
2 **Be going to** introduces *a prediction / a plan.*

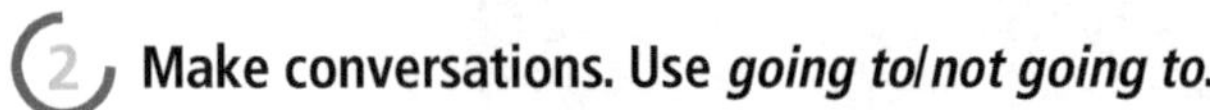

2 Make conversations. Use *going to/not going to.*

1 **A** What / you / do on the weekend?
B I / buy a new T-shirt.
What are you going to do on the weekend?
I'm going to buy a new T-shirt.
2 **A** It's jeans day tomorrow. What / you / wear?
B Well, I / not wear my school uniform!
3 **A** They / take up / a collection for charity.
B I / not make / a donation. I don't have any money.
4 **A** You / sign the petition against the new supermarket?
B Yes, I am. I don't agree with it.
5 **A** My brother / be a volunteer at the school marathon.
B What he / do?
6 **A** You / take a banner to the march?
B Yes, I am. I / write a slogan on it, too.

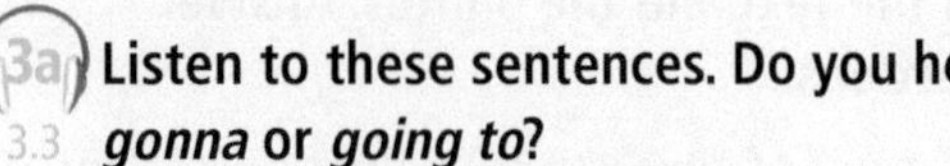

Pronunciation Going to

3a 3.3 **Listen to these sentences. Do you hear *gonna* or *going to*?**

1 I'm going to play football.
2 We're going to a concert.
3 What time is it going to start?
4 Are you going to the party?

b 3.3 **Listen again and repeat.**

4 3.4 **Complete the conversation. Then listen and check.**

A Hey, Connor. [1] *Are you gonna play* (you/play) football in the park on Saturday?
B No, I'm not. I [2] .... (make) a banner.
A What for?
B Sunday is Earth Day. There [3] .... (be) a march.
A Earth Day? [4] .... a lot of people .... (go)?
B Yes, they are. And after the march, we [5] .... (have) a concert in the park.
A That's cool. Who [6] .... (play)?
B Taylor Swift and Lorde.
A Wow! What time [7] .... (start)?
B At three o'clock. [8] .... (you/come)?
A Yes, I am!

5 Imagine you are organizing a concert for a charity. In pairs, ask and answer.

1 Which charity / help?
2 Which group / play?
3 the concert / be at school?
4 What time / begin and end?
5 How / make money? you / sell T-shirts, CDs?

Which charity are you going to help?

We're going to help the World Wildlife Fund.

• *Will* or *be going to*

Predictions

In 30 years there won't be any Asian elephants.
You'll probably meet one near the beach this weekend.

Plans or intentions

We're going to save the Asian elephant.

Grammar reference page 122

Look at the sentences. Are they plans or predictions?

1 Your horoscope says, "The color red will bring you good luck." *prediction*
2 I'm not going to go to school tomorrow—it's Saturday!
3 We're going to go to the basketball game this weekend. We've bought our tickets.
4 I don't think he'll pass his exams. He never does his homework.
5 My friend has problems with math, so I'm going to help him after school.
6 I'm sure we'll have fun at the party. Everyone will be there.

Complete the sentences. Use *will* and *going to*.

1 I / do my homework now. Maybe I / call my friends later.
I'm going to do my homework now.
Maybe I'll call my friends later.
2 We / play baseball on Saturday. We hope we / win.
3 He / get a bike for his birthday. Maybe it / be red.
4 Lola is sick. She / not go school today. Perhaps she / feel better tomorrow.
5 We / watch a DVD tonight. I hope it / be a scary movie.
6 I / not go to the charity event. Maybe people / not notice.

Vocabulary • Verb + preposition

Look at the phrases. Check the meaning of each in a dictionary. Listen and repeat. 3.5

agree with	apologize for	argue with
believe in	care about	decide on
disapprove of	hope for	insist on
know about	protest against	worry about

Word list page 61 **Workbook** page 130

Match the beginnings (1–6) to the endings (a–f) of the sentences.

1 She apologized *a*
2 We have to decide
3 I don't believe
4 Everyone hopes
5 Do you know
6 On his birthday Aidan insisted

a for her bad behavior.
b in charity. People should help themselves.
c for a better world.
d about the party on Saturday night?
e on getting a pet snake.
f on a topic for our school project.

Complete the text. Use the correct prepositions.

Walk around the Barrio Gótico in Barcelona and you'll see strange marks on the street. They say "city residents" on one side and "tourists" on the other. People are worried [1] *about* the number of tourists in the city, and the marks show people are protesting [2] .... this. Many people agree [3] .... the protest. "Sometimes I can't cross the street because there are so many tourists," says Nuria Cugat. "They're noisy and rude. They don't care [4] .... our city." Julio Sanchez disapproves [5] .... the protest. "I can't argue [6] .... Nuria about the noise, but we need tourism."

In pairs, ask and answer.

1 How often do you argue with your parents?
2 Do you worry about exams?
3 What things do you care about?
4 Have you ever protested against something?

Brain Trainer Unit 7
Activity 3
Go to page 64

Chatroom Persuading

Speaking and Listening

1 Look at the photo. Answer the questions.

1 Where are the teenagers?
2 What do you think they are doing?
3 What do the slogans on their T-shirts say?
4 What do you think Ella is saying to Ruby?

2 Listen and read the conversation. Check your answers. 3.6

3 Listen and read again. Answer the questions. 3.6

1 Why are they protesting?
The city council is going to close down the library.
2 What does Ella want Ruby to do?
3 Why can't Ruby join them?
4 What does Ella say they have?
5 What does Ash say Ruby can do?
6 Why does Tom think the demonstration is important?

4 Act out the conversation in groups of four.

Ruby Hi, guys. What are you doing here?
Tom We're protesting.
Ruby What are you protesting against?
Ash The city council is going to close down the library. They say that people don't use it, but that's not true!
Ella Will you sign our petition? If you sign it, you'll help to keep the library open.
Ruby I suppose so.
Tom Hey, why don't you join us?
Ruby Sorry, I can't. I have homework to do.
Ella Come on, Ruby. It'll be fun. Look, we have T-shirts with slogans.
Ash And you can hold my sign. It's better than doing homework.
Ruby I don't know.
Tom But it's important. We all use the library, and we care about what happens to it. If we don't protest, they *will* close it. I'm sure you don't want that to happen.
Ruby OK, I'll do it. You win! Where's my T-shirt?!

Say it in your language …

Come on.
I suppose so.
You win!

5 Look back at the conversation. Who says what?

1 Come on, Ruby. *Ella*
2 It'll be fun.
3 It's better than doing homework.
4 I'm sure you don't want that to happen.

Persuading	Responding
Come on. It'll be fun.	I don't know.
It's better than ... + *ing*.	OK, I'll do it.
I'm sure you ...	

6 Read the phrases for persuading and responding.

7 Listen to the conversation. What is Ruby persuading Tom to do? In pairs, act out the conversation.

3.7

Tom This is [1] hard!
Ruby Come on, Tom. It'll be fun.
Tom I don't know. This is the first time I've [2] been on a skateboard. I'm going to [3] fall!
Ruby No, you're not. I'm sure you'll be fine.
Tom OK, you win! ... Hey, this is easier than I thought.
Ruby Yes, and it's better than [4] playing soccer!

8 Work in pairs. Replace the words in purple in Exercise 7. Use these words and/or your own ideas. Act out the conversations.

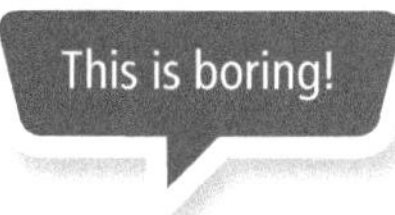

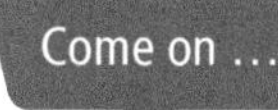

1 hard / dangerous / tiring

2 played the guitar / ridden a scooter / trained for a marathon

3 hurt my fingers / fall / stop after 5 km

4 listening to music / playing a computer game / going for a bike ride

Grammar • First conditional

if + Present simple, *will* + infinitive
If we don't protest, they will close the library.
will ('ll) + infinitive > *if* + Present simple
They will close the library if we don't protest.

Grammar reference page 122

1 Study the grammar table. Choose the correct options to complete the rules.

1 We use the First conditional to talk about *possible / impossible* situations.
2 The Present simple after *if* refers to events in *the future / the present*.

2 Complete the sentences.

1 If I *buy* (buy) a new T-shirt, it *won't have* (not have) a slogan.
2 You .... (not pass) your exam if you .... (not review) your notes.
3 If you .... (care about) your friend, you .... (help) him.
4 He .... (laugh) if you .... (tell) him a joke.
5 If we .... (have) a school sit-in, there .... (be) trouble!
6 She .... (have) fun if she .... (go) to the fundraising event.
7 If they .... (be) worried about the library, they .... (sign) the petition.
8 I .... (get) angry if you .... (argue) with me.

3 Complete the sentences in your own words.

1 If I save some money, ...
2 If I have some time tonight, ...
3 If it's sunny this weekend, ...
4 If I have a birthday party, ...
5 If we go on vacation, ...

4 In pairs, ask and answer about your sentences in Exercise 3.

What will you do if you save some money?

I'll buy a new watch.

Reading

1 **Look at the title of the magazine article and the photos. What do you think the article is going to be about?**

Eco World

Do Something Different ...

You don't have to go on a march or sign a petition to make a difference and change things. This week in *Eco World* magazine, we look at other ways you can protest.

350.org

350.org is an organization that protests against climate change. It believes that if you do something different, more people will listen. In 2010 it organized the world's biggest art exhibition, called eARTh. People in sixteen different countries made huge pictures on the ground outside. You could only see the pictures from satellites in space.

In the Delta del Ebro in Spain, an artist named Jorge Rodriguez-Gerada created a picture of a little girl named Galla. Galla was worried about global warming, and the picture is about what might happen to the Ebro River. Hundreds of volunteers helped Jorge make it, and thousands of people have seen it on Google Earth™.

Critical Mass bike rides

On a Friday evening in September 1992, sixty cyclists met in San Francisco and went on a bike ride. There was a lot of traffic on the roads, but there were a lot of bikes too, so cars stopped for them. This was the world's first Critical Mass bike ride. Cyclists on the ride were protesting against cars and pollution. They wanted safer roads for cyclists.

Today over 200 cities have CM bike rides. Rides take place on the last Friday of every month, and there are often more than 1,000 cyclists. The protests have made a difference, and many cities now have bicycle lanes and "car free" days. This year the biggest bike ride will be on Earth Day in Budapest. "There are going to be 80,000 people on 80,000 bikes!" says one cyclist. Imagine that!

Key Words

organization climate change traffic pollution bicycle lanes

2 (3.8) **Read the article. Copy the table and match the organizations to the things they are protesting against.**

cars	~~climate change~~
dangerous roads	environmental damage
global warming	pollution in cities

350.org	CM bike rides
climate change	

3 **Read the article again. Answer the questions.**

1 How does 350.org believe you can make people listen?
If you do something different, more people will listen.
2 What was unusual about the art exhibition?
3 What did Jorge Rodriguez-Gerada do?
4 Where was the first CM bike ride?
5 Why did cars stop for the bikes?
6 How have the CM protests made a difference?

4 **Think about protests that have happened in your country. Choose one example.**

1 What was the problem?
2 How did people protest? What did they do?
3 Did the protest make a difference?

Listening

1 (3.9) **Listen to the radio interview about a charity. Answer the questions.**

1 Who does Link Romania help?
2 What does it do?

Listening Bank Unit 7 page 67

Writing • A formal letter

1 Read the Writing File.

Writing File Letter writing

When you write a letter or email to a magazine, you can use these phrases.

- **Opening**
  Dear (+ name of person or magazine),
- **Say why you are writing**
  I am writing to comment on …
- **Closing**
  Kind regards, (+ your name)
  Best wishes, (+ your name)

2 Read the letter. Match the parts (1–5) to (a–e).

a reason for writing
b opening the letter *1*
c closing the letter
d What action can we take?
e What is the problem?

Eco World Letters Page

1 Dear Eco World,

2 I am writing to comment on your article about biking to school in this week's magazine. In the article, you say not many kids bike. I think this is because there are not enough bicycle lanes. Kids don't feel safe on a bike, so most of them go to school by car (including me!).

3 If people don't bike, there will be more traffic on the roads, and more pollution. This is bad for the environment.

4 How can we encourage people to get on their bikes? The solution is clear: we need more bicycle lanes. If we sign a petition asking for bicycle lanes, maybe the city council will listen. If there are more lanes, more kids will bike to school!

5 Kind regards,

Samantha Kippel

3 Read the letter again. Answer the questions.

1 Why is Samantha writing to *Eco World*?
She wants to comment on an article about biking.
2 Why don't kids bike to school?
3 Why is this bad for the environment?
4 What does Samantha suggest?

4 Match these problems (1–4) to the headlines (a–b) from *Eco World*.

1 There won't be a place for kids to play.
2 We won't have a place to study.
3 There won't be a place for people to read.
4 We won't have a place for people to walk.

a Park Is Going, Parking Lot Is Coming!

Our local park is going to become a parking lot. A lot of people use the park—there's a children's play area and a café there.

b Library Is Going to Close

The city council has decided to close our library. They say that the library is too expensive.

5 Choose one article from Exercise 4. Take notes about the problems. Try to think of a solution.

6 Write a letter to *Eco World* about the article you chose in Exercise 5. Use "My formal letter" and your notes from Exercise 5.

My formal letter

1 **Opening**
Dear Eco World,
2 **Reason for writing and the problem**
I am writing to comment on the article about …
In the article, you say that …
3 **Action**
How can we save our …?
4 **Closing**
Kind regards,/Best wishes,

Remember!

- Use phrases from the Writing File.
- Use the vocabulary in this unit.
- Check your grammar, spelling and punctuation.

Refresh Your Memory!

Grammar • Review

1 Complete the sentences. Use *going to* and these verbs.

have	not go	not watch
~~review~~	send	wear

1 I *'m going to review* my notes tonight. I have an exam tomorrow!
2 We .... the concert this weekend. We don't have tickets.
3 .... they .... a picnic? It's a beautiful, sunny day.
4 He .... the football game. He hates football!
5 .... she .... invitations to the party?
6 It's cold outside. .... you .... a coat?

2 Complete the sentences. Use *will* or *going to* and the verbs.

1 Maybe I*'ll wear* (wear) a dress to the party. I don't know.
2 Brett is wearing his bike helmet. He .... (ride) his bike.
3 Let's go on a boat ride. Maybe we .... (see) a dolphin.
4 She .... (go) skiing this winter. She's booked a hotel in the Alps.
5 Maybe it .... (be) sunny later. Then we can go to the beach.
6 I .... (watch) my favorite TV show tonight. It starts at 7.

3 Match the beginnings (1–6) to the endings (a–f) of the sentences.

1 If we sign the petition, *f*
2 If she says "sorry,"
3 If they go shopping,
4 He won't be happy
5 If I tell you the truth,
6 You'll get a sunburn

a will you be friends again?
b if his team loses.
c will you keep it a secret?
d they'll buy some new clothes.
e if you lie in the sun too long.
f we'll make a difference.

Vocabulary • Review

4 Choose the best options.

1 There's a *march* / *sit-in* today. It starts downtown and ends at the park.
2 I gave $5 to UNICEF today. Have you ever made a *donation* / *collection* to a charity?
3 It was a successful *petition* / *fundraising event*. We took in $5,000 for the hospital!
4 I like the *slogan* / *banner* on your T-shirt. "Save the Planet" is cool!
5 The WWF is *a charity* / *a collection* that helps animals.
6 Protestors were carrying *signs* / *slogans* with *signs* / *slogans* on them. They said, "Save Our Jobs!"

5 Complete the sentences with these words.

agree	apologized	argue	care
insists	know	~~protested~~	worried

1 A lot of people *protested* angrily against the new highway.
2 I .... for forgetting my homework.
3 Do you .... about endangered animals?
4 I'm not .... about my exams. I know I'll do OK.
5 Do you .... with me?
6 Do you .... about Zoe's party this weekend?
7 I never .... with my girlfriend.
8 Our teacher always .... on silence in class.

Speaking • Review

6 3.10 **Put the conversation in the correct order. Then listen and check.**

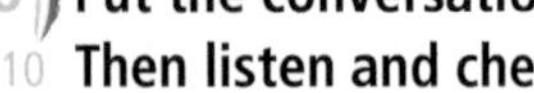

Girl I don't want to make these banners. I'm bored. *1*
Boy No, it won't. I'm sure we'll finish them quickly.
Girl OK, you win! It's better than doing it on my own.
Boy Come on, I'll help you. It'll be fun.
Girl I don't know. There's a lot of work to do. It's going to take a long time!

Dictation

7 3.11 **Listen and write in your notebook.**

My assessment profile: page 143

Global Citizenship File

FAIRTRADE: CHOCOLATE

1 What is it?

Shopping connects us with millions of people around the world. These people work on farms and in factories, and they make the things we buy. Many of them come from developing countries, and big companies don't pay them much money.

Fairtrade companies give people a fair price for the work they do. They help people take care of their families and buy the things they need. They also make sure that people work in safe conditions. Sometimes you pay a little more for Fairtrade products, but if we pay a little more, people in other countries will have better lives.

Fairtrade Fact File: Chocolate

2 ....

Chocolate comes from cocoa beans on cocoa trees. Cocoa trees grow in countries with a tropical climate. Cameroon, Ivory Coast and Ghana all grow cocoa beans. Countries like these are often very poor.

3 ....

Cocoa farmers grow the cocoa beans. Many farmers earn less than fifty cents a day. They grow their own food, but it's hard for them to pay for other things, like medicine and clothes.

4 ....

Farmers get more money for their work, so they can buy medicine and send their children to school. Some villages now have access to clean water, too. Farmers also get help and advice about farming. They learn new skills, so they become better farmers.

5 ....

- Find Fairtrade chocolate at your local supermarket, then vote with your wallet and buy it!
- Encourage your friends and family to do the same.
- Make your school Fairtrade-friendly. Design a poster, or start a petition.
- Ask for Fairtrade products (not just chocolate!). There are more than 3,000 Fairtrade products to choose from!

Key Words

farms	factories
developing country	fair price
tropical climate	vote

Reading

1 Read the article quickly. Match the headings (A–E) to the paragraphs (1–5).

A What is it? *1*
B Who makes it?
C How does Fairtrade help?
D What can we do?
E Where is it from?

2 Read the article again. Are these statements true (T) or false (F)? 3.12

1 Big companies pay people more money. *F*
2 Fairtrade products are sometimes more expensive than other products.
3 Countries that grow cocoa beans are usually rich.
4 Cocoa farmers have to pay for their food.
5 Fairtrade helps farmers improve their work.
6 There aren't many Fairtrade products.

My Global Citizenship File

3 Choose another Fairtrade product and take notes about it. Think about:

- where it is from
- who grows or makes it
- how Fairtrade helps
- what we can do to help

4 Write a Fairtrade fact file about your product. Add photos or pictures. Use your notes from Exercise 3 to help you.

Danger and Risk

Grammar
Second conditional;
Relative pronouns

Vocabulary
Extreme adjectives;
Illness and injury

Speaking
Talking about health

Writing
An application form

Word list page 61
Workbook page 131

Vocabulary • Extreme adjectives

1 (3.13) **Listen and repeat. Then match the normal adjectives (1–10) to the extreme adjectives in the box. Check your answers in a dictionary.**

awful
burning
~~excellent~~
exhausted
freezing
furious
huge
terrifying
thrilled
tiny

a

1 good *excellent*
2 small
3 hot
4 cold
5 scary
6 big
7 bad
8 pleased
9 angry
10 tired

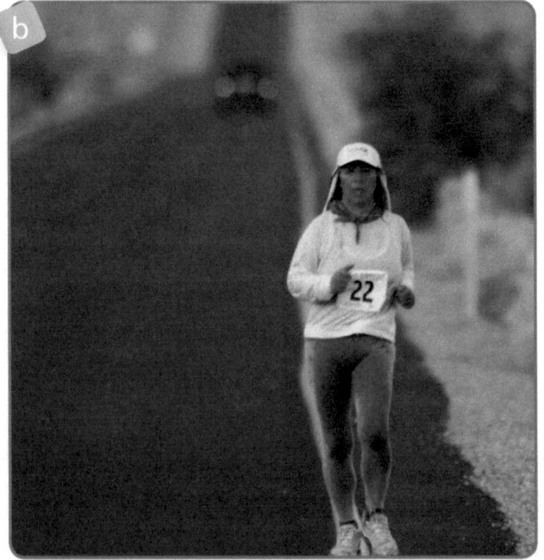

b

2 **Match the comments (1–3) to the photos (a–c).**

1 It's huge and he's tiny. It looks freezing cold.
2 It's an excellent picture. It looks terrifying.
3 It's an awful place. I think she's exhausted.

c

3 (3.14) **Complete the conversations with extreme adjectives. Listen and check, then practice with a partner.**

A Was the movie really good?
B It was [1] *excellent*.

A Are you very tired?
B Yes, it's late. I'm [2]..... .

A Brr! It's really cold in here.
B You're right. It's [3]..... . Do you have a sweater?

A Is he really pleased with his grade on the exam?
B He's [4]..... . He did really well.

A Was your mom really angry that you stayed out late?
B Yes, she was. She was [5].... !

4 What about you? **In pairs, ask and answer.**

Have you ever …
- watched a terrifying movie?
- gotten an excellent grade on an exam?
- picked up a huge spider?

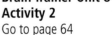

Brain Trainer Unit 8
Activity 2
Go to page 64

Reading

1 **You are going to read about an unusual job. Before you read, look at the photo and answer the questions.**

1 What type of job do you think it is?
2 How do you think the person feels?
3 Why do you think she does it?

2 **Read the interview quickly and check your answers.**

3 **Work in pairs. Find these numbers in the interview. What do they refer to?**

- 80
- 1,000,000
- 8
- 100

4 3.15 **Read the interview again. Are these statements true (T) or false (F)?**

1 In today's movies, computers create most of the stunts. *F*
2 Stunts can be very expensive.
3 Naomi doesn't earn much money.
4 She was tired after her first job.
5 She has had a lot of accidents.
6 She thinks a police officer's job is more dangerous.

5 **In pairs, ask and answer.**

1 Do you think Naomi's job is dangerous?
2 Can you think of other dangerous jobs?
3 Do you know anyone who does a dangerous job?
4 Would you like to be a stuntman or woman? Why?/Why not?

Interview: Naomi Daniels

Interview

Naomi Daniels

Today's action movies are often thrilling adventures with amazing stunts. Computers create some of these stunts, but stuntmen and stuntwomen do most of them. In some action movies, there are more than eighty stuntmen and women, and one stunt can cost over a million dollars! It's an exciting job, but what about the risks? We interviewed stuntwoman Naomi Daniels.

Naomi, why are you a stuntwoman?
Because it's an excellent job! I earn a lot of money, I travel around the world, I meet famous people, and I never do the same thing twice. If I weren't a stuntwoman, I'd do extreme sports. But stunts are more fun!

Can you remember your first job?
Yes, I can. It was a car race in the desert. It was burning hot, and it took eight hours to film. At the end of the day, I was exhausted.

Do you ever worry about the risks?
Sometimes, but I practice a lot, and I'm very careful. I don't usually have accidents, but last year I hurt my leg. I was furious because it was an easy stunt—a jump from a hundred-meter-high bridge!

If I were you, I'd be really frightened!
Well, if I were scared, I wouldn't be a stuntwoman.

Would you be happier if you had an ordinary job?
No, I wouldn't. If I had an ordinary job, I'd be bored. And I don't think my job is dangerous. When I see police officers or firefighters, then I think, "Wow, that's dangerous."

Grammar • Second conditional

if + Past simple, *would ('d)* + verb *would ('d)* + verb > *if* + Past simple
Affirmative
If I had an ordinary job, I'd be bored.
Negative
If I weren't a stuntwoman, I'd do extreme sports. If I were scared, I wouldn't be a stuntwoman.
Questions and short answers
Would you be happier if you had an ordinary job? Yes, I would./No, I wouldn't.

Watch Out!
If I were you, I'd be terrified.
= If I ~~was~~ you, I'd be terrified.

Grammar reference page 124

1 Study the grammar table. Choose the correct options to complete the rules.

1 We use the Second conditional to talk about *probable / improbable* situations or *real / unreal* events.
2 The Past simple after *if* refers to events now or *in the future / in the past*.

2 Choose the correct options.

1 If I could choose any job, I *would be / will be* a firefighter.
2 If I *forgot / forget* my friend's birthday, I would feel embarrassed.
3 He would be furious if you *copied / copy* his homework.
4 If we learned another language, we *studied / would study* Chinese.
5 I would wear a big coat if it *is / were* freezing outside.
6 If she went to bed late, she *is feeling / would feel* exhausted.
7 It *will be / would be* awful if they had an accident.
8 If I could meet anyone in the world, it *would be / will be* Justin Bieber.

3 Complete the text with the correct form of the verbs.

If you [1] *had* (have) tickets for a huge, terrifying roller coaster ride, what [2].... (you/do)? "I'd go on it," says Joel Alvaro. "If I [3].... (can) ride roller coasters all day, I [4].... (do) it," he adds, "but I have to go to work." Joel is a teacher—he also loves amusement parks. "If I [5].... (live) in Orlando, Florida, I [6].... (be) thrilled," he says. Orlando has the most roller coaster rides in the world! If he [7].... (be) in Orlando, he [8].... (visit) Disney World every day. But he doesn't. His girlfriend thinks he's crazy. "Roller coasters are fun, but if I [9].... (go) on them all the time, I [10].... (get) bored and feel sick!" she says.

4 Look at these situations. Make questions.

1 
2 
3 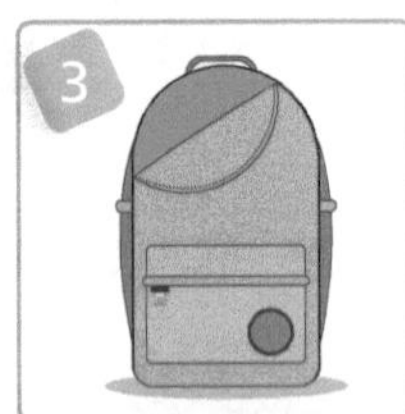
4 
5 
6 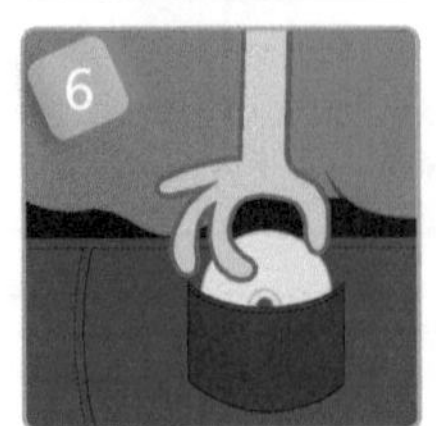

1 you / see / a movie star
What would you do if you saw a movie star?
2 you / find / 50 dollars in the street
3 you / lose / your backpack
4 your friend / break / your cell phone
5 your parents / be / furious with you
6 your friend / steal / from a store

5 In pairs, ask and answer the questions in Exercise 4.

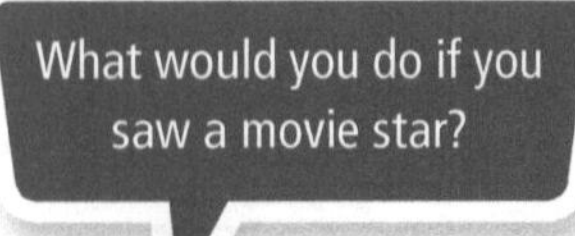
What would you do if you saw a movie star?

I'd ask him or her for an autograph.

Vocabulary • Illness and injury

1 3.16 **Match the pictures (1–12) to these words and phrases. Then listen, check and repeat.**

a backache	a burn	a cold
a cough	a cut	a fever
a headache	a rash *1*	a sore throat
a sprained ankle	a stomachache	a toothache

Word list page 61
Workbook page 131

2 **What's wrong with these people?**

1 My head hurts. I'm going to take an aspirin.
a headache
2 I fell down the stairs, and now I can't walk.
3 I can't eat anything. There's something wrong with my tooth.
4 I can't stand straight or lift heavy things.
5 My head feels hot, but I feel cold. I need a blanket.
6 I ate too much. I feel sick.
7 I had an accident. I hurt my finger with a knife.

3 **Complete the sentences with the words in Exercise 1.**

1 He spilled boiling water on his hand, and now he has a really bad *burn*.
2 My nose is red, and I don't feel very well. I think I have a.... .
3 My.... is so bad it wakes me up at night.
4 I have a.... . It hurts when I eat or drink.
5 This.... is awful. I can't stop scratching!

Pronunciation *gh*

4a 3.17 **Listen and repeat. How do we pronounce *gh* in these words?**

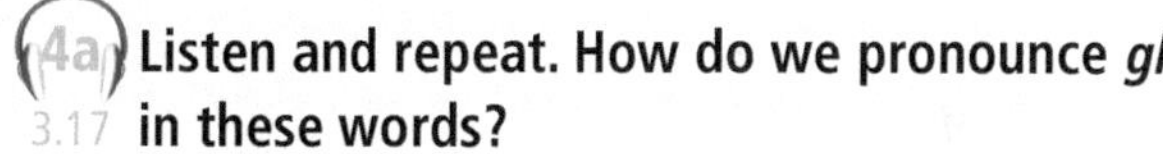

brought	cough	eight	enough
high	laugh	rough	thought

b 3.18 **Copy the table and put the words in Exercise 4a in the correct column. Then listen and check.**

/f/	silent
cough	*brought*

c 3.19 **Listen and repeat. Pay close attention to the *gh* sound.**

1 It's eight o'clock.
2 Have you had enough to drink?
3 I brought some medicine for your cough.
4 Don't laugh. I thought you were sick!

Brain Trainer Unit 8
Activity 3
Go to page 65

Chatroom Talking about health

Speaking and Listening

1 Look at the photo. Answer the questions.

1 Where are Tom and Ruby?
2 What's wrong with Ruby?
3 What did Tom do?

2 Listen and read the conversation. Check your answers. 3.20

3 Listen and read again. Answer the questions. 3.20

1 How did Ruby hurt herself?
She tripped over a cat.
2 Where was the woman?
3 What does Tom do at the O_2 arena?
4 How did Tom hurt himself?
5 What does he think is wrong?
6 Why does Ruby feel sorry for Tom?

4 Act out the conversation in pairs.

Tom	Hi, Ruby. What's the matter?
Ruby	Oh, I hurt my arm.
Tom	How did you do that?
Ruby	Well, I tripped over a cat which ran out from under a car.
Tom	That's awful!
Ruby	The cat was OK, but my arm wasn't. The woman who was in the car brought me here. Oww!
Tom	Are you all right?
Ruby	Don't worry, I'm fine. So why are *you* here?
Tom	I had a silly accident at the O_2 arena.
Ruby	The what?
Tom	The O_2 arena, you know … it's the place where I play soccer.
Ruby	So what happened?
Tom	I was trying to score a goal when I fell over the ball.
Ruby	That's funny, except your leg looks terrible. How does it feel?
Tom	Not too good. I think I have a sprained ankle. And we lost the game!
Ruby	Poor thing!

Say it in your language …
That's awful!
Poor thing!

Look back at the conversation. Complete the sentences.

1 *What's* the matter?
2 I.... my arm.
3 Are you.... ?
4 I'm.... .
5 .... does it feel?

Read the phrases for asking and talking about health.

Asking about health	Responding
What's the matter?	I have a headache/ a sprained ankle/ a toothache, etc.
Are you all right?	I'm fine, thanks.
How does it feel?	Not too good./Pretty bad.
How do you feel?	A little better, thanks.

3.21 **Listen to the conversations. What's wrong with Tom and Ella? Act out the conversations in pairs.**

Ash Hi, Tom. You look awful! What's the matter?
Tom Achoo! I have [1] a cold.
Ash Poor thing! How do you feel?
Tom Not too good.

Ella I feel awful. I have [1] a headache.
Ash Can I get you anything?
Ella No, I'm fine, thanks. … OK, maybe [2] a hot drink.
Ash You should [3] get some rest, too.

8 Work in pairs. Replace the words in purple in Exercise 7. Use these words and phrases and/or your own ideas. Act out the conversations.

1 a backache / a sprained ankle / a toothache

2 a hot water bottle / some ice / some medicine

3 go to the doctor / take an aspirin / go to the dentist

Grammar • Relative pronouns

It's the place where I play soccer.
She's the woman who was in the car.
That's the cat which was under a car.

Grammar reference page 124

Study the grammar table. Complete the rule with *who, which* or *where*.

We use relative pronouns to talk about places (....), people (....) and things (....).

Choose the correct options.

1 I don't like stories *who* / *which* make me cry.
2 That's the store *which* / *where* I got my shoes.
3 This is the bag *which* / *who* is very heavy. The others are OK.
4 There's the beach *where* / *which* we went swimming last year.
5 She's the girl *who* / *which* is good at soccer.
6 That's the TV show *which* / *who* is all about doctors.

Complete the sentences with *who, which* or *where*.

1 I hate movies *which* are scary.
2 He's someone.... is very kind.
3 It's the place.... we went for Tom's birthday.
4 Those are the jeans.... were very expensive.
5 That's the pizza place.... I usually go.
6 She's the teacher .... is always late.

Complete the conversation with *who, which* or *where*.

A There's the boy [1] *who* won the competition.
B Oh, really? Where was that?
A It was at the skatepark [2].... is near the beach.
B I don't know it.
A Well, it's the place [3].... I go on weekends.
B Is it good?
A Yes. It has a café [4].... you can meet friends. Look! He's walking this way.
B Is he the tall one?
A No. He's wearing a black T-shirt [5].... has a cool slogan.
B Ah yes! There's a girl [6].... is talking to him. She's holding a cell phone [7].... has a pink cover.
A That's right. Hmm … is she his girlfriend?

Reading

1 Look at the photo. Answer the questions.

1 What's happening in the photo?
2 How does the girl feel? How would you feel?
3 Why do you think people take risks?

This Week's **Big Question**

Why Are People Risk-Takers?

Recently amazing teenagers have been in the news. Laura Dekker has sailed around the world, Parker Liautaud has skied to the North Pole, and Amelia Hempleman-Adams has skied to the South Pole. These teenagers are all natural risk-takers, but why do they do it? We looked at some popular explanations.

1 It's all about adrenalin

Some scientists believe that risk-takers' bodies don't react to danger like most people's bodies. When we are in danger, our bodies make a chemical called adrenalin. It stimulates our brain and makes us ready to fight or run away. Risk-takers' bodies don't make adrenalin easily, so they take more risks to feel "alive."

2 Little old women don't go snowboarding

Studies have shown that tall people take more risks than small people, women are more careful than men, and older people take fewer risks than younger people. Tall people are often confident, and confident people are not easily scared. Scientists also think that men are more natural risk-takers than women, and that age and experience make people more cautious … or really boring!

3 Be careful what you watch

Recent research asked these questions, too. If you played a computer game about risk-taking, would that make you take risks in real life? And if your parents or friends took risks, would you take them, too? It seems the answer to both questions is yes!

And finally … some researchers say that risk-takers are frequently bored—they often change jobs, and they don't have long relationships. But some people say they are happier. What do you think?

Key Words

risk-taker	scientist	react
stimulate	research	

2 Read the magazine article and check your answers to Exercise 1.

3 Find these words in the article. In pairs, try to explain what they mean. Look them up in a dictionary to check.

1 chemical (line 16)
2 confident (line 31)
3 cautious (line 37)
4 frequently (line 50)

4 Read the article again. Answer the questions. 3.22

1 What do the teenagers in the introduction have in common? *They are all risk-takers.*
2 Why do risk-takers take risks?
3 Why do tall people take more risks?
4 What happens when we get older?
5 How do risk-takers often feel?

5 In groups, discuss these questions.

1 Are you tall, young and healthy?
2 Do you ever feel scared?
3 Do you love computer games?
4 Are you a risk-taker? Why?/Why not?

Listening

1 Listen to two people talking about a TV show. Answer the questions. 3.23

1 What's the show called?
2 Name two things the teenagers have to do.
3 What's the prize?

Listening Bank Unit 8 page 67

Writing • An application form

1 **Read the Writing File.**

Writing File Completing an application form

- Read the questions: do you have to write information or choose an answer?
- If you have to write information, what kind of information is it? (name, date, number?)
- If you have to choose an answer, read all the answers first.
- Complete the form.
- Check what you have written.

2 **Read the application form for the *Survivor* TV show. Complete the questions with these words.**

how (x2)	how many	what
where	why	

Survivor

Application Form

Send your application form to:
Survivor
51 W 52nd St
New York, NY 10019

Name *Casey MacDonald* Age *14*

1 .... adventurous are you? (5 = very, 1 = not at all)
1 ☐ 2 ☐ 3 ☐ 4 ☑ 5 ☐

2 .... of the activities have you done? (mark the boxes)
camping ☑ climbing ☑ sailing ☐ fishing ☑ cooking ☐

3 If you could visit *one* of these places, ... would you go? Mark the box. Say why.
the jungle ☐ a desert island ☐ Disney World ☑
I'd like to go to Disney World because I love roller coasters, and it would be really exciting.

4 .... would your best friend describe you? Circle four words.
(adventurous) nervous (funny) serious (happy) moody (friendly) shy

5 .... are you scared of?
I'm terrified of losing.

6 .... do you want to be on *Survivor*?
Because I love trying new things. I also want to be on TV!

3 **Match the question words (1–6) to the answers (a–f). What type of information do the answers give (e.g., a number, a date, a place, a person, a reason, a thing)?**

1 What *f*
2 Who
3 How many
4 Where
5 When
6 Why

a Because it's my birthday.
b On Friday, June 12.
c My friends.
d At the pizza place.
e Twelve.
f A party.

4 **Read the application form again. Answer the questions.**

1 Which activities has Casey never tried?
sailing and cooking
2 Where would he like to go?
3 Is he a confident person?
4 What is he worried about?
5 Why does he want to be on the show?

5 **Copy and complete the application form for you.**

Remember!

- First, read the questions: do you have to circle or mark an answer, or write information?
- If you have to write information, what kind of information is it?
- If you have to choose an answer, read all the answers first.
- Complete the form.
- Check what you have written in the form carefully.
- Use the vocabulary in this unit.
- Check your grammar, spelling and punctuation.

Refresh Your Memory!

Grammar • Review

1 Complete the sentences. Use the Second conditional.

1 If she *didn't have* (not have) homework, she'd watch the action movie.
2 .... (he/travel) abroad if he had more time?
3 They.... (climb) the mountain if it stopped snowing.
4 If you.... (be) famous, would you be my friend?
5 What.... (you/do) if you lost your cell phone?
6 If people.... (not take) risks, would they be happier?

2 Read the sentences. Are the explanations (a and b) true (T) or false (F)?

1 If I could sing, I'd be a pop star.
  a I can sing very well. *F*
  b I can't sing at all. *T*
2 If he went on the roller coaster, he'd enjoy it.
  a He probably won't go.
  b He's going to go.
3 If she worked hard, she'd be at the top of her class.
  a She works hard.
  b She doesn't work hard.
4 If they were good at basketball, they'd be on the school team.
  a They are on the school team.
  b They aren't on the school team.
5 I'd be furious if you broke my MP3 player.
  a You probably won't break it.
  b The MP3 player doesn't work.
6 If I could meet anyone in the world, I'd choose Lady Gaga.
  a You'll probably never meet her.
  b You're going to meet her next week.

3 Choose the correct options.

1 A nurse is a person *who* / *which* takes care of people.
2 The movie theater is a place *which* / *where* we can watch movies.
3 There's the girl *which* / *who* was late for class.
4 Swimming is a sport *who* / *which* is good for you.
5 Isn't that the hotel *which* / *where* we stayed?
6 This is the café *where* / *who* I meet my friends.
7 I like this bag—the one *who* / *which* is $55.

Vocabulary • Review

4 Replace the words in bold with extreme adjectives.

awful	~~exhausted~~	freezing	furious
huge	terrifying	thrilled	tiny

1 I've studied all day. I'm **really tired**! *exhausted*
2 The burger was **very big**, but he ate it all.
3 Dad was **really angry** when I broke his watch.
4 The bird was **very small**. I held it in my hand.
5 My sister Jenny was **very pleased** with her birthday present.
6 I didn't enjoy the party. The music was **very bad**.
7 It's **really cold** outside. It has started to snow.
8 The horror movie was **very scary**.

5 Match the illnesses and injuries to the definitions.

a cold	~~a fever~~	a headache
a sore throat	a sprained ankle	a stomachache

1 This makes you feel hot and cold. *a fever*
2 Your nose is sore.
3 This hurts when you walk.
4 Your stomach hurts.
5 Your throat hurts.
6 Your head and eyes hurt.

Speaking • Review

6 3.24 **Complete the conversation with these words. Then listen and check.**

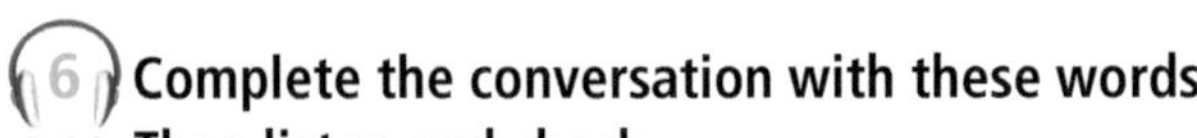

~~all right~~ feel get have how too good

Girl You look awful! Are you [1] *all right*?
Boy No, I'm not [2].... . I [3].... a stomachache.
Girl Poor thing! Can I [4].... you anything?
Boy Maybe a glass of water.
Girl Here you go. [5].... do you [6].... now?
Boy A little better, thanks.

Dictation

7 3.25 **Listen and write in your notebook.**

My assessment profile: page 144

Real World Profiles

Crina "Coco" Popescu's Profile

Age	Home country
18 years old	Romania

My favorite things ...

climbing, biking, running, swimming, travel, my family and friends

Coco Loves Climbing

In 2011 Crina "Coco" Popescu climbed Mount Sidley, the highest mountain in Antarctica. The views from the top of the mountain were amazing, but the most amazing thing was Coco's age: she was only 16. Today Coco is 18, and she is also the youngest woman to climb the seven highest volcanoes in the world.

Coco started climbing when she was six years old. First, she climbed the mountains around her hometown of Rasnov. Then she started to climb bigger, more dangerous mountains. When she was 10, she climbed the huge Dente del Gigante mountain in the Alps. After the climb, she was exhausted, but also excited ... about her next challenge!

So how does she do it? Well, she works very hard. Coco trains every day after school. She also goes running, swimming and biking. If she didn't train, she wouldn't be strong enough to go on expeditions. She doesn't have much time to watch movies, shop or go out with her friends.

Coco is an excellent climber, but she doesn't take risks. In 2009 she was halfway up a mountain in the Himalayas when the weather suddenly changed. It was a dangerous situation and a terrifying experience. She gave up the expedition and went home. Coco was disappointed, but she learned from her ordeal. Today, with the help of her family and friends, she's broken six world records. "I can't thank my parents enough for their support," says Coco. "I'm trying hard to make them proud."

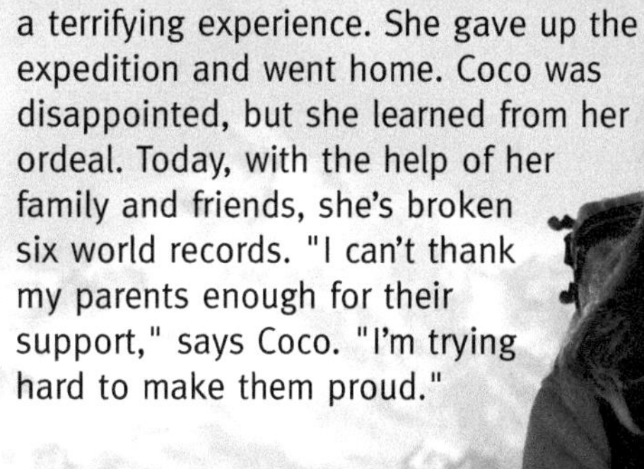

Reading

1 Read Coco's profile. Correct the mistakes in this short text.

Coco is a 16-year-old climber from Romania. Besides climbing, Coco loves biking and skateboarding, and she's also a good swimmer. She doesn't like traveling much, but she loves her family and friends.

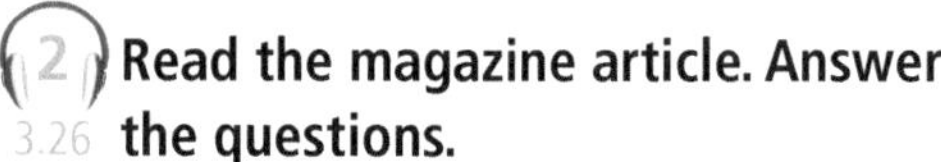

2 Read the magazine article. Answer the questions. 3.26

1 What did Coco do when she was 16?
She climbed the highest mountain in Antarctica.
2 When did she start climbing?
3 How did she feel after climbing the Dente del Gigante?
4 How is her free time different from her friends' free time?
5 Why did she give up on the Himalayan mountain?
6 How many world records has she broken?

Class discussion

1 Are there any young record breakers like Coco in your country?
2 Are there any mountains in your country? If there are, which is the highest?
3 Which is the highest mountain in the world? Which country is it in?

9 Inventions

Grammar
Present simple passive;
Past simple passive

Vocabulary
Machine nouns and verbs;
Word building

Speaking
Problems with machines

Writing
An opinion essay

Word list page 61
Workbook page 132

Vocabulary • Machine nouns and verbs

1 3.27 **Match the pictures (1–8) to these verbs. Then match the pictures (9–18) to these nouns. Then listen, check and repeat.**

Verbs: attach build communicate *1* invent plug in press produce turn on/off

Nouns: battery button cable jack keyboard outlet power cord remote control tube *10* wheel

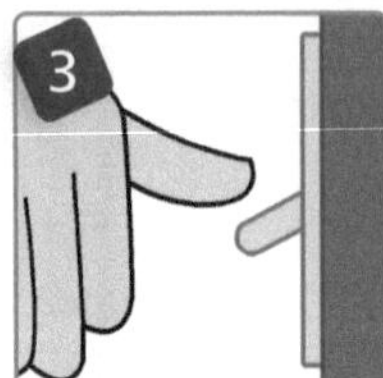

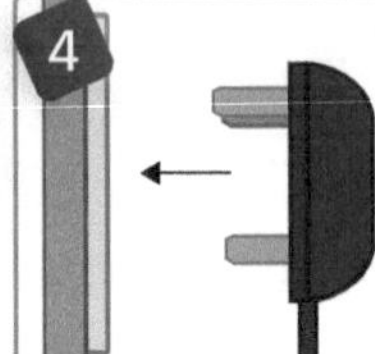

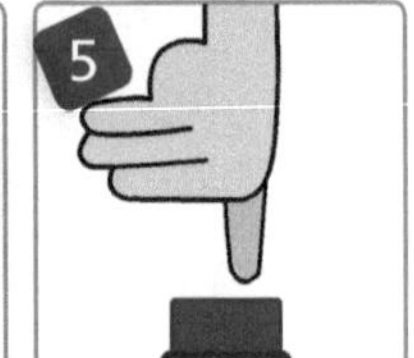

2 **Look at the machine and complete the instructions. Use the words in Exercise 1.**

MY MARVELOUS ICE CREAM MAKER

[1] *Plug* the power cord into the nearest [2] .... .
[3] .... the red button to [4] .... the machine.
Put eggs, cream and sugar into the different [5] .... s.
Use the [6] .... on your laptop to write the name of your favorite ice cream.
Turn the [7] .... or press the [8] .... s on the [9] .... .
The machine will [10] .... some tasty ice cream.
Remember to [11] .... the machine.
Then enjoy!

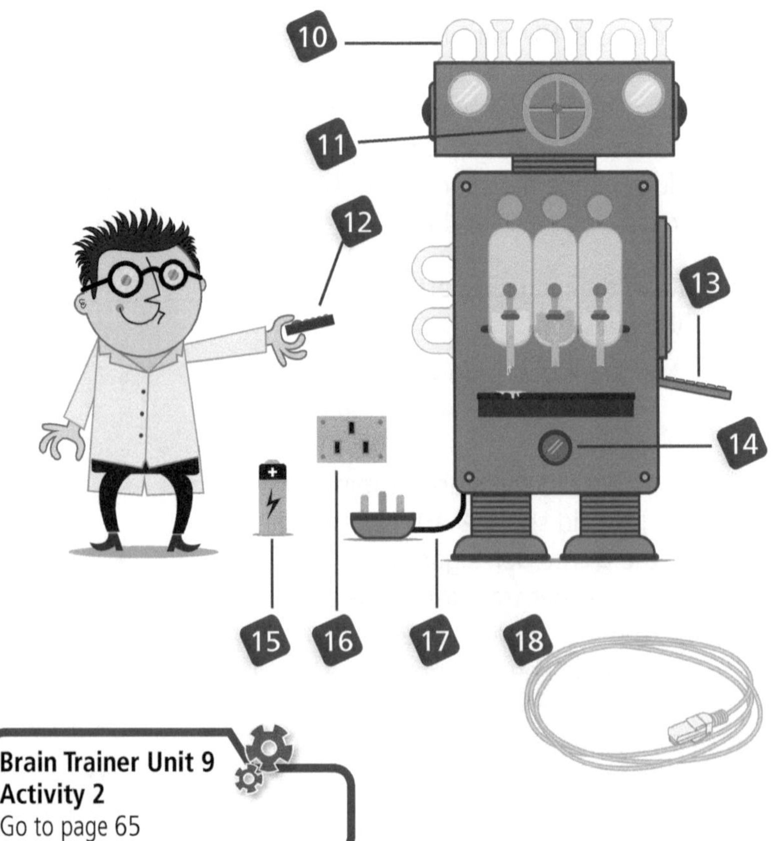

3 **In pairs, take turns describing one of these things. Use words from Exercise 1 and the words below.**

cell phone flash drive flashlight tablet train TV

A *It has a battery. Before you can use it, you have to turn it on. You can use it to produce light and to see in the dark.*
B *It's a flashlight!*

Brain Trainer Unit 9 Activity 2
Go to page 65

Reading

1 **Think of some famous inventors. What did they invent?**

2 **Read the magazine article quickly. Match the paragraphs (1–3) to the photos (a–c).**

3 **Read the article again. Are these statements true (T) or false (F)?**
3.28

1 Louis Braille could never see. *F*
2 His system of writing was a completely new idea.
3 Alexander Kendrick's invention can help people with injuries.
4 People should always have a cell phone with them when they are spelunking.
5 Hibiki Kono's invention uses machines that many people have in their homes.
6 He uses his invention to climb the walls in his bedroom.

4 **What do you think?**

1 Which of the inventions in the photos is
a the smartest?
b the most useful?
c the most fun?
Say why.

> I think the low-frequency radio is the smartest invention. It's difficult to build a radio, and this radio can do things that other radios can't do.

2 If you were an inventor, what would you invent?

> I would invent a robot that could do all my homework for me!

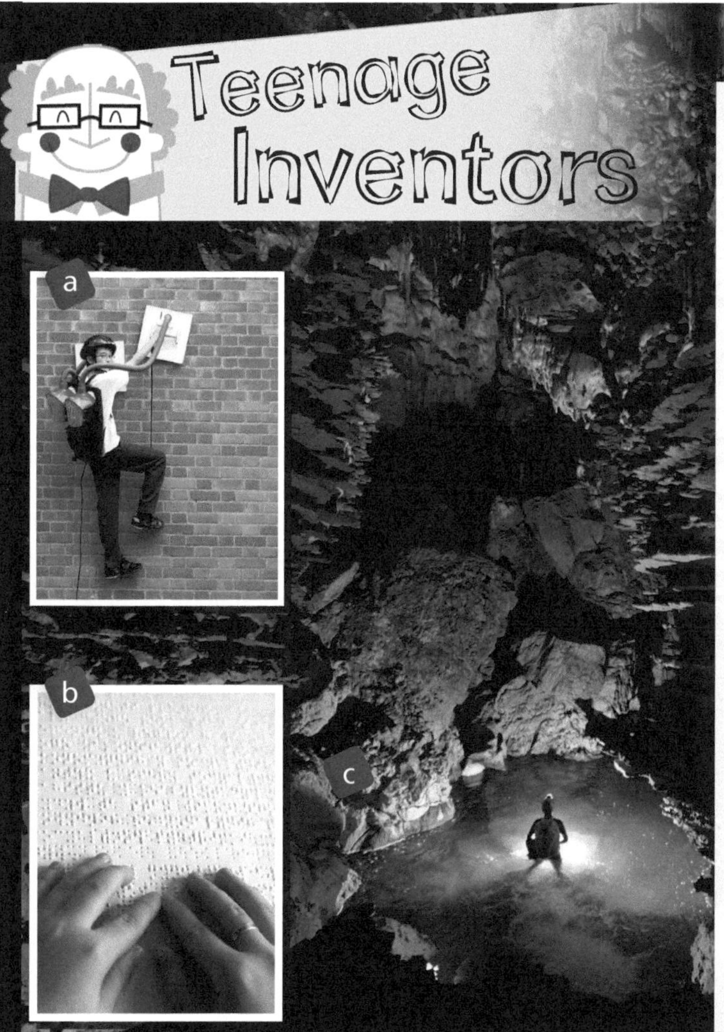

You don't have to be old with crazy white hair to invent something. Here are some of our favorite young inventors.

1 Louis Braille (1809–1852) was French. He became blind in an accident when he was only three years old. At the age of twelve, he learned about a system of writing with bumps in paper that you feel with your fingers. Louis liked this idea, but the writing was difficult to read. For the next three years, he worked on a similar, but easier system. The result of his work was "Braille" writing. The first book in Braille appeared in 1829, and Braille is still used by blind people today.

2 Sixteen-year-old Alexander Kendrick loves spelunking, but it's a very dangerous activity. When accidents happen underground, it's impossible to communicate with the outside world. Messages that are sent on traditional radios or cell phones can't travel through rock. Alexander has built a special low-frequency radio that works 300 meters underground. It is made with plastic tubes and metal cable, and messages are written on a keyboard. This clever machine might save a lot of lives in the future.

3 Gloves aren't usually used to climb walls, are they? Well, thirteen-year-old Hibiki Kono has invented special gloves! A small vacuum cleaner is attached to each glove. When the vacuum cleaners are turned on, the gloves can carry the weight of a large person on a wall or ceiling. But Hibiki isn't allowed to use the gloves in his bedroom. His mom thinks they're too dangerous.

Grammar • Present simple passive

Affirmative
It is made with plastic tubes. They are made with plastic.

Negative
The machine isn't made with plastic. Gloves aren't usually used to climb walls.

Questions and short answers
Is the machine made with plastic? Yes, it is./No, it isn't. Are the gloves used to climb walls? Yes, they are./No, they aren't.

Grammar reference page 126

1 Study the grammar table. Choose the correct options to complete the rules.

1 We use the passive when we want to focus on *the action / the person or thing doing the action.*
2 We make the Present simple passive with the Present simple of *have / be* and the Past participle.

2 Complete the sentences with the Present simple passive of the verbs.

A lot happens around the world in one minute:
1 A hundred new cars *are produced* (produce).
2 The Internet .... (use) by 64 million people.
3 Twelve million text messages .... (send).
4 10,000 songs .... (download) from the Internet.
5 1.5 million kilograms of trash .... (throw away).

3 Make sentences.

1 our washing machine / run / every day
Our washing machine is run every day.
2 the cables / not plug in / to the right jacks
3 My laptop isn't working. My homework / not save / on another computer!
4 batteries / not include

4 Make questions. Then ask and answer in pairs.

1 cell phones / allow / in class?
Are cell phones allowed in class?
2 interactive whiteboards / use / at your school?
3 English / speak / all the time in your English class?
4 your TV / turn on / all evening?

• Active and passive

Active
Blind people use Braille. You write messages on a keyboard.

Passive
Braille is used by blind people. Messages are written on a keyboard.

Grammar reference page 126

5 Study the grammar table. Choose the correct options to complete the rules.

1 With an active verb, the person or thing that does the action goes *before / after* the verb.
2 With a passive verb, we *always / don't always* mention the person or thing that does the action.
3 With a passive verb, we introduce the person or thing that does the action with *by / for.*

6 Change these active sentences into passive sentences. Don't include *by* + noun.

1 People spend seventy-five billion dollars on video games every year.
Seventy-five billion dollars *are spent on video games every year.*
2 People eat a lot of ice cream in the summer.
A lot of ice cream .... .
3 They don't sell that candy in my town.
That candy .... .
4 Teachers give too much homework to students.
Too much homework .... .

7 Change these active sentences into passive sentences. Include *by* + noun.

1 A hairstylist usually cuts my hair.
My hair *is usually cut by a hairstylist.*
2 The average teenager sends almost nine hundred text messages every month.
Almost nine hundred text messages .... .
3 A Japanese company makes those cell phones.
Those cell phones .... .
4 The sun warms the water in the pool.
The water in the pool is .... .

Vocabulary • Word building

1 Take the quiz.

2 Listen and check.
3.29

1 **What did Coco Chanel design?**
a *clothes*
b planes
c computers

2 **What is Pablo Picasso's *Guernica*?**
a a film
b a book
c a painting

3 **What was Alexander Graham Bell's most famous invention?**
a the phone
b the radio
c the TV

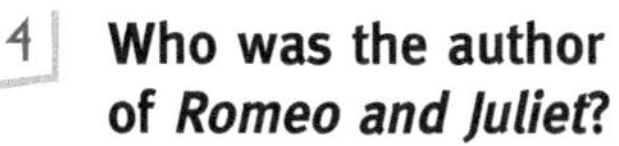

4 **Who was the author of *Romeo and Juliet*?**
a Charles Dickens
b William Shakespeare
c Agatha Christie

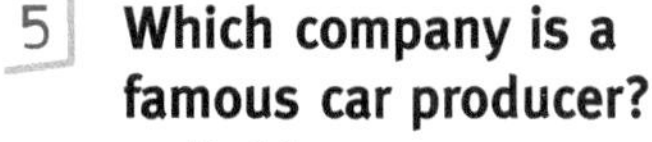

5 **Which company is a famous car producer?**
a Nokia
b Ikea
c Volvo

6 **What is the Taj Mahal?**
a a mountain
b a building
c a river

3 Copy and complete the table.

verb	noun 1: person	noun 2: result
build	builder	1 *building*
2	designer	design
invent	inventor	3 ....
paint	painter	4 ....
produce	5	product
write	6	writing

Word list page 61
Workbook page 132

4 Complete the text with these words.

built	designs	inventor
~~painted~~	painter	paintings

Leonardo da Vinci 1 *painted* the *Mona Lisa*, one of the world's most famous 2 .... . But he wasn't only a 3 .... . He was also the 4 .... of flying machines, musical instruments and hundreds of other things. Some experts have followed his 5 .... for a flying machine and have 6 .... one that can fly!

Pronunciation /ɪ/ and /i/

5a Listen and repeat.
3.30

big	build	clean	email
Internet	keyboard	silly	wheel

b Copy the table and put the words in Exercise 5a in the correct column. Then listen and check.
3.31

/ɪ/	/i/
big	*clean*

c Listen and repeat.
3.32
1 The D on his keyboard disappeared.
2 Build a bigger machine, please.
3 She invented a new, thinner screen.

Brain Trainer Unit 9
Activity 3
Go to page 65

Chatroom Problems with machines

Speaking and Listening

1 **Look at the photo. What do you think the girls are doing?**

2 **Listen and read the conversation.**
3.33 **Check your answer.**

3 **Listen and read again. Complete the sentences.**
3.33
1 What did Ella make the robot from?
An aluminum can.
2 What did she find on the Internet?
3 What's the problem with the robot?
4 How does Ella know that the battery is OK?
5 Why didn't she see the red button before?
6 How does the robot break?

4 **Act out the conversation in pairs.**

Ruby Is that your robot for the science project? It's so cute! Was it made from an aluminum can?
Ella Yes, it was. But it doesn't work.
Ruby What's the problem?
Ella Well, the instructions weren't included in the box. I found some on the Internet, and I've done everything that they say, but the wheels don't move.
Ruby There might be something wrong with the battery. Have you checked it?
Ella Yes. It was only bought yesterday, and it works OK in my flashlight.
Ruby Have you tried pressing that red button?
Ella No, I haven't—it was hidden under the robot's arm. Here goes … Yay! It's working!
Ruby Watch out, Ella! It's going to fall off the table!
CRASH!
Ella Oh no! It's broken. What am I going to do now?

Say it in your language …
It's so cute!
Here goes.
Yay!

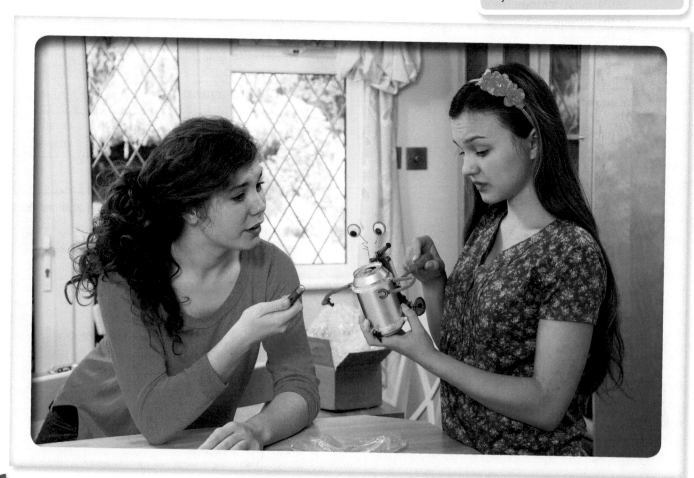

5 **Look back at the conversation. Complete the sentences.**

1 It doesn't *work*.
2 What's the .... ?
3 Have you .... it?
4 Have you .... pressing that red button?

6 **Read the phrases for talking about problems.**

Talking about problems with machines	
What's the problem?	It doesn't work. It's broken. The (wheels) don't (move).
Have you tried (pressing that button)?	No, I haven't.
There might be something wrong with the battery. Have you checked it?	

7 3.34 **Listen to the conversation. What does Ash suggest? Act out the conversation in pairs.**

Ash Let's [1] watch this DVD on your laptop.
Tom We can't. [2] It doesn't work.
Ash What's the problem?
Tom [3] The laptop can't play it.
Ash There might be something wrong with [4] the DVD. Have you checked it?
Tom Yes. It works OK [5] in the DVD player.
Ash Have you tried [6] restarting your laptop?

8 **Work in pairs. Replace the words in purple in Exercise 7. Use these words and/or your own ideas. Act out the conversation.**

Let's watch TV.

We can't. It doesn't work.

1 listen to some music / send Ruby a text
2 my MP3 player / my cell phone
3 there is no sound / it can't send texts
4 the "play" button / the battery
5 and it says "playing" / and I charged it earlier
6 turning it off and on again / standing outside in the yard

Grammar • Past simple passive

Affirmative	Negative
It was made by Ella.	It wasn't made by Ella.
They were bought yesterday.	The instructions weren't included in the box.
Questions	
Was it made from an aluminum can? Yes, it was./No, it wasn't. Were the instructions included? Yes, they were./No, they weren't.	

Grammar reference page 126

1 **Study the grammar table. Choose the correct option to complete the rule.**

We form the Past simple passive with the Past simple of *be* / *have* and the past participle.

2 **Complete the text with the Past simple passive form of the verbs.**

The first cell phones were very big. They [1] *were used* (use) on trains and planes in the 1920s. A cell phone network [2] .... (introduce) in Tokyo in 1979, and other cities soon followed. The first text message [3] .... (send) in Finland in 1993, and later, cell phones [4] .... (produce) that could take photos and use the Internet. In 2010 more than five billion cell phones [5] .... (own) by people around the world!

3 **Change these sentences into the passive. Only include *by* + noun if this is important.**

1 People in the US invented the Internet.
The Internet was invented in the US.
2 Da Vinci didn't build the world's first plane.
3 My friend Jack won the science fair.
4 They didn't tell the students about the exams.
5 My dad designed our house.

4 **Make questions in the Past simple passive. Then ask and answer.**

1 your favorite photos / take / on a cell phone?
Were your favorite photos taken on a cell phone?
2 your favorite book / write / a long time ago?
3 your favorite movies / make / in your country?
4 your class / give / a lot of homework last week?

Reading

1 Look at the photos (a–d). Put the inventions in the order that they were invented.

A Book for All Time?

Next time you hold a book in your hands, stop and think. Like most other things in the modern world, it is the result of thousands of years of human invention.

First came the invention of writing, probably about 5,500 years ago. With writing, people did not have to remember everything in their heads. They could communicate with people that they never saw and share their knowledge with future generations.

Later, the Greeks were known throughout the ancient world for their literature, philosophy and science, but their "books" looked very different from the books of today. They were called scrolls. They were difficult to use and took up a lot of space in a library. It was only about 2,000 years ago that books with a lot of pages were invented. With the help of an index at the back, readers could find information more quickly than in a scroll. Before long, scrolls were a thing of the past.

For more than a thousand years, the pages of books were made from animal skin. That changed in the thirteenth century, when Europeans learned about a useful Chinese invention: paper.

But the biggest change for books came around 1439, when Johannes Gutenberg invented the printing press. Before that, books were copied by hand, so they were very expensive. Many more people could afford the books that were produced on a printing press.

These days it is difficult to imagine a world without books. But human invention does not stop. Every year, more stories are bought as e-books and read on a screen.

Will anyone turn the pages of a traditional book in the future, or will books, like scrolls, soon disappear?

Key Words

knowledge	generation	ancient
index	skin	traditional

2 Read the magazine article quickly to check.

3 3.35 **Read the article again. Are these statements true (T) or false (F)?**

1 The ancient Greeks invented writing. *F*
2 Greek books had a lot of pages.
3 There were libraries in the ancient world.
4 The first books with pages were made of animal skin.
5 Paper was invented in Europe.
6 Gutenberg's printing press made cheaper books.

4 3.35 **Read the article again. Answer the questions.**

1 What did people have to do before the invention of writing?
They had to remember everything in their heads.
2 What two problems were there with scrolls?
3 Why were books easier to use than scrolls?
4 What did people use to make books when they stopped using animal skin?
5 For what reasons was the printing press an important invention?
6 Why might books disappear in the future?

Listening

1 What are the advantages and disadvantages of reading on a smart phone?

2 3.36 **Listen to the conversation. Do they talk about any of your ideas in Exercise 1?**

Listening Bank Unit 9 page 67

3 In pairs, ask and answer.

1 Do you like these types of stories?
- fantasy
- funny
- historical
- horror
- romantic
- science fiction

2 How many books do you read every year?
3 Do you prefer traditional books or e-books? Why?
4 Will books exist in fifty years? Why?/Why not?

I like funny stories, but I don't like horror or science fiction stories.

Writing • An opinion essay

1 **Read the Writing File.**

Writing File How to write an opinion essay

In an opinion essay, you need:

- **a title**
- **an introduction giving your opinion** *(In my opinion, …)*
- **reasons for your opinion, given in a good order** *(First, … , Second, … , Finally, …)* **with examples** *(for example, …)*
- **a conclusion** *(In conclusion, …)*

2 **Read Alisha's essay. Find words and expressions from the Writing File.**

The Most Useful Invention for Teenagers

by Alisha Kent

In my opinion, the most useful invention for teenagers is the smart phone.

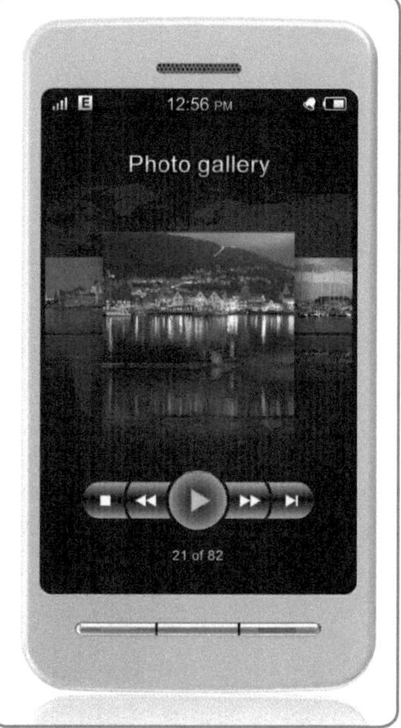

First, it's great in an emergency. If someone has an accident or there's a fire, you can call quickly for help. Because of this, parents often feel more relaxed if you have a smart phone with you, and you can stay out longer with your friends.

Second, you can use it to go online when you aren't at home. This is useful in many situations. For example, you can find out the time of the next bus when you're in a café, and look at a map on the Internet when you're lost.

Finally, a smart phone is great entertainment. You can watch movies on it, play games, listen to music and read stories. With a smart phone in your pocket, you never have to be bored, even on a long trip.

In conclusion, the smart phone is a fantastic invention. Teenagers are happier and more independent because of it.

3 **Put these parts of an opinion essay in the correct order.**

a In conclusion, Edison's inventions were some of the most useful in the world.
b Second, he invented a way to bring electricity to people's homes.
c In my opinion, the world's greatest inventor was Thomas Edison.
d The World's Greatest Inventor *1*
e First, he invented the lightbulb.
f Finally, he invented a machine that could record and play sound.

4 **Read Alisha's essay again. Answer the questions.**

1 In Alisha's opinion, what is the most useful invention? *The smart phone.*
2 Why did she choose this invention?
3 In what two situations is it useful?
4 How are teenagers' lives different because of it?

5 **You are going to write an essay with this title:**

The most important invention of the last 200 years

Choose an invention and take notes about it. Use the questions in Exercise 4 to help you.

• car • computer • Internet • plane • TV

6 **Now write your essay. Use "My essay" and your notes from Exercise 5.**

My essay 

Paragraph 1
Introduce the invention.
Paragraphs 2–4
Give reasons why it is important—one reason for each paragraph. Include examples of situations that prove your point.
Paragraph 5
Summarize your reasons for choosing this invention.

Remember!

- Give an introduction with your opinion.
- Give reasons for your opinion.
- Write a conclusion.
- Use words you've practiced in this unit.
- Check your grammar, spelling and punctuation.

Refresh Your Memory!

Grammar • Review

1 Complete the sentences with the correct passive form (Present simple or Past simple) of the verbs.

1 She *was interviewed* (interview) on the news yesterday.
2 Excuse me! .... (dogs/allow) on the bus?
3 I can't read that. It .... (write) in French.
4 .... (the Internet/use) in the 1950s?
5 That word .... (not spell) correctly. Use a dictionary!
6 Too many trees .... (cut down) every year.
7 The dishes .... (not do) last night.
8 Skateboards .... (invent) in the US in the 1950s.

2 Make sentences and questions in the passive. Only use *by* + noun if necessary.

1 They play football in the park every Saturday.
Football is played in the park every Saturday.
2 Do people read books at your school?
3 James broke my pen.
4 They don't speak Japanese in Thailand.
5 My grandma made this sweater.
6 We didn't need the tent.
7 Did they make these computers in China?
8 Our friend designed the website.

3 Active or passive? Complete the text with the correct form of the verbs.

In 1901 American inventors Wilbur and Orville Wright [1] *built* (build) a flying machine, but it [2] .... (not design) well enough. It [3] .... (not fly)! "Man will fly, but not in our lifetime," Wilbur [4] .... (say) sadly.
The brothers [5] .... (learn) from their mistakes, however. In 1903 some changes [6] .... (made) to the design, and a new machine [7] .... (build). Wilbur [8] .... (carry) through the air for 59 seconds in the new machine. Some photos [9] .... (take) of this famous moment—the first flight of the world's first plane! Today the names of the Wright brothers [10] .... (know) all around the world, and thousands of people [11] .... (come) to see their plane at the museum in Washington where it [12] .... (keep).

Vocabulary • Review

4 Match the beginnings (1–8) to the endings (a–h) of the sentences.

1 You can write on your computer with a
2 Plug the cable into the
3 The flashlight won't work without a
4 A bicycle has two
5 Please don't press those
6 You can turn on the TV with a
7 Posters are often sold in a
8 Plug the power cord into the

a tube.
b audio jack.
c remote control.
d wheels.
e keyboard.
f outlet.
g battery.
h buttons.

5 Complete the sentences with the correct form of the words.

1 Claude Monet was a famous French *painter* (paint).
2 What .... (produce) is Apple™ famous for?
3 Her .... (write) is difficult to read.
4 I love his .... (design) for the new school building.
5 The .... (build) has to put a new roof on the house.
6 Everyone thinks it's a useful .... (invent).

Speaking • Review

6 3.37 **Complete the conversation with the correct form of these words. Then listen and check.**

check go ~~not work~~ problem try wrong

Dad It's time to practice your electric guitar!
Boy I can't. It [1] *isn't working*.
Dad What's the [2] .... ?
Boy It can only play really quietly. Listen!
Dad There might be something [3] .... with the cord. Have you [4] .... it?
Boy But it's new. It was bought yesterday.
Dad Er … Have you [5] .... plugging it in?
Boy Yikes! I forgot! Here [6] .... . Yay! It's working!

Dictation

7 3.38 **Listen and write in your notebook.**

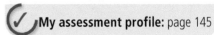

My assessment profile: page 145

Science File

Did you know that 0.039% of the gas in the Earth's atmosphere is carbon dioxide (CO_2)? CO_2 is a greenhouse gas: it absorbs infrared radiation. Because of this, too much CO_2 in the atmosphere causes global warming.

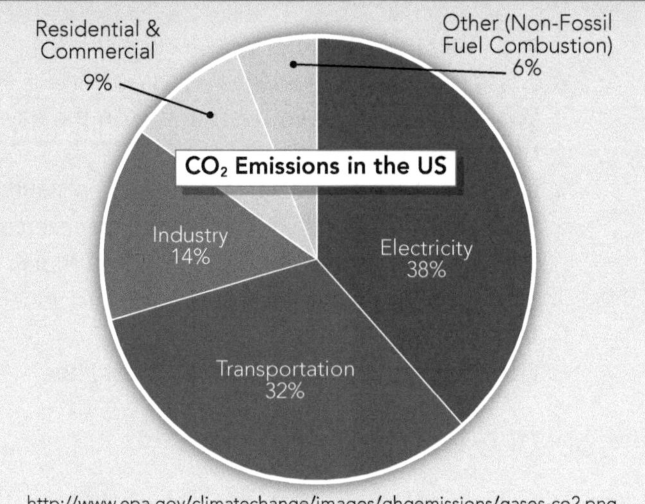

http://www.epa.gov/climatechange/images/ghgemissions/gases-co2.png

CO_2 is produced when fossil fuels are burned. The average person in the United States causes 17.6 metric tons of carbon dioxide emissions every year (see chart). The world average is 4.95 metric tons. If our emissions continue, many islands and lowland areas might disappear under the ocean, many parts of the world might become desert, and the plants and animals that live in the oceans and on ice might die.

CO_2 is absorbed by trees and changed into oxygen. However, the average tree absorbs only 10 kg of CO_2 in a year. We would need 1,760 trees per person to absorb all our CO_2 emissions, but there are only 59 trees per person in the world. Every year 25 million trees are cut down, and only 3.4 million trees are planted.

The average modern car produces 15% less CO_2 than a car that was built 10 years ago. Many new water heaters, computers and other machines also produce less CO_2 than older designs. But we use more hot water, drive farther and switch on our machines for longer each year, so we are producing more CO_2, not less.

Key Words

atmosphere, absorb, fossil fuel, heater, greenhouse gas, infrared radiation, emission

Reading

1 3.39 **Read the text and look at the chart. Are the statements true (T) or false (F)?**

1 Americans cause more CO_2 emissions than the world average. *T*
2 Industry causes more CO_2 emissions than transportation.
3 Trees change CO_2 into oxygen.
4 There are more people in the world than trees.
5 New car designs produce more CO_2 than old ones.
6 We produce less CO_2 than we did in the past.

2 3.40 **Liam is giving a presentation to his class. Listen and match his notes (1–4) to a–d.**

What could I do to produce less CO_2 when I travel?

1 My car's emissions:
2 If I rode my bike to soccer practice:
3 If we took three friends to school in our car:
4 If I got up early on Mondays:

a 1.6 kg less CO_2 per week
b 15 kg less CO_2 per week
c 600 g less CO_2 per week
d 200 g of CO_2 per km

My Science File

3 **Find out what you can do to produce less CO_2 in one of these areas.**

- around the house
- communication
- entertainment
- food
- travel

4 **Prepare a presentation for the class, giving your ideas for producing less CO_2. Then give your presentation.**

Grammar • Be going to

1 Make questions and answers.

1 What / you / do / next weekend?
What are you going to do next weekend?
2 I / play tennis.
3 Karen / clean the house.
4 Jo and Ross / do judo.
5 They / not / do any housework.
6 Maria / not / study.
7 What / Mom / make for dinner?
8 She / not / cook.
9 We / go out / for dinner!
10 you / have a pizza?

• *Will* or *be going to*

2 Complete the sentences with *will* or *be going to.*

1 I've decided what to give Mom for her birthday. I*'m going to* buy her some flowers.
2 It .... rain, I think. Look at those clouds.
3 **A** Do you think you .... be famous one day?
4 **B** Yes! Because I .... be a really successful pop singer!
5 **A** Where .... to go for summer vacation?
6 **B** I .... go to Thailand.
7 **A** How .... I know when you get there?
8 **B** I .... send you a text message!
9 **A** The menu looks good. Have you decided what you .... have?
10 **B** Hmm. I think I .... have the chicken pot pie.

• First conditional

3 Complete the First conditional sentences. Use the correct form of the verbs.

1 If I*'m* (be) free tonight, I*'ll call* (call) you.
2 I .... (give) him the message if I .... (see) him.
3 What .... (happen) if you .... (be) sick on the day of the exam?
4 If it .... (rain), we .... (not sit) outside at the restaurant.
5 You .... (not get) fit if you .... (not do) any exercise.
6 I .... (text) you if you .... (give) me your number.
7 Where .... (you go) if you .... (not get) into your first-choice college?
8 I'm sure she .... (help) you if you .... (ask) her.

• Second conditional

4 Make Second conditional questions and answers.

1 What / you do / if you / see / someone stealing?
What would you do if you saw someone stealing?
2 If I / see someone stealing / I / call the police.
3 I / lend you my bike / if I / have one.
4 If Carrie / work harder / she / pass her exams.
5 If you / come home late, your parents / be angry?
6 I / walk away / if someone / be / rude to me.
7 If it / not raining / I / go for a walk.
8 What / you do / if you / forget / your mom's birthday?
9 If I / forget my mom's birthday / I / be sad.

• Relative pronouns

5 Complete the sentences. Use *where, which* or *who.*

1 These are the shoes *which* were expensive.
2 The woman .... is in the hospital is our teacher.
3 The sandwich .... I made was delicious.
4 Picasso is the artist .... painted that picture.
5 That's the café .... we go on weekends.
6 The suitcase .... is heavy is mine!
7 The dog .... barks all the time is annoying.
8 Memphis is the city .... we saw a basketball game.

• Present simple passive

6 Complete the sentences with the Present simple passive form of the verbs in parentheses.

1 Every day, millions of text messages *are sent*. (send)
2 The winners .... after the contest. (announce)
3 The windows .... every two months. (clean)
4 In our school, students who misbehave .... detention. (give)
5 Ice cream .... from milk. (make)
6 Every season a new football team captain .... . (choose)
7 A lot of the world's olive oil ... in Spain. (produce)
8 How often .... complaints about customer service .... ? (receive)

• Past simple passive

7 Make sentences in the Past simple passive.

1 When / pizzas / first / invent?
When were pizzas first invented?
2 Where / the first Olympic Games / hold?
3 What / yo-yos / first / use for?
4 Why / the Globe Theater / rebuild?
5 The airport / close / because of bad weather.
6 The criminal / send / to prison.
7 I / give / some money for my birthday.
8 you / invite / to their wedding?

Speaking • Persuading

1 Complete the conversation with these words.

be fun	better than	~~come on~~
don't know	I'll do	sure you

A I don't feel like going to the tango dancing class tonight.
B Oh, [1] *come on*, Alice! It'll [2] .... !
A I [3] .... . I'm terrible at dancing.
B I'm [4] .... aren't. Anyway, we're all beginners. Please come. It'll be [5] .... staying at home all alone.
A OK. [6] .... it. Just don't laugh at me when I fall!

• Talking about health

2 Put the conversation in the correct order.

.... No, I'm fine. I'll just rest here for a little while.
..*1*.. Oww!
.... I can see that by the way you're walking ... Here, sit down for a second. How does that feel?
.... What's the matter, Rosie?
.... A little better, thanks.
.... Maybe you sprained it. Should I call the doctor?
.... I have a pain in my knee all of a sudden.

• Problems with machines

3 Make the conversation.

1 **A** I / borrow your digital camera?
Can I borrow your digital camera?
2 **B** Sorry, / it / not / work.
3 **A** What / problem / with it?
4 **B** There / might / something / wrong / battery.
5 **A** you / check / it?
6 **B** Yes, I / have.
7 **A** you / try / take / it out? And putting it back in again?
8 **B** No, I / haven't. I / try / that now.

Review 3

Vocabulary • Protest and support

1 Choose the correct option.

1 Please sign our *banner* / *petition*. We are collecting signatures of people who are against the proposed new freeway.
2 The roads are closed because of a large student *demonstration* / *donation*.
3 We are making *signs* / *charities* to hold up when we go on the *sit-in* / *march* through the streets.
4 The *slogan* / *collection* of our protest movement is, "Do you call this progress?"
5 We're organizing a *sit-in* / *fundraising event* for a *banner* / *charity* called Children in Need.
6 We need people to distribute pamphlets about our organization. Would you like to be a *sign* / *volunteer*?
7 Please make a generous *slogan* / *donation* to our *collection* / *petition* for blind people.

• Verb + preposition

2 Complete the sentences with the correct prepositions.

1 I'm sorry, I don't agree *with* you.
2 Do you care .... the environment?
3 The government insists .... going ahead with its plans for a new airport.
4 I apologize .... my late arrival.
5 Do you ever worry .... the future?
6 What are the students protesting .... ?
7 We all hope .... a solution to the problem of global warming.
8 Do you argue .... your parents about grades?

• Extreme adjectives

3 Complete the sentences with extreme adjectives.

1 It wasn't just small—it was *tiny*.
2 It was really cold—.... , in fact.
3 We weren't just tired after the hike. We were .... .
4 The movie was more than good. It was .... .
5 It wasn't just scary—it was .... .
6 Bad? It was much worse than that. It was absolutely .... .

• Illness and injury

4 Choose the correct option.

1 I ate too much, and now I have a *sprained ankle* / *stomachache*.
2 I need to go the dentist. I have a *toothache* / *headache*.
3 Look at these spots all over my arms. It's some kind of *cough* / *rash*.
4 Your *burn* / *fever* is very high—look, it shows 39°C on the thermometer.
5 I have a *backache* / *sore throat*—it really hurts when I eat.
6 I have a bad *cold* / *cut* on my finger. It's bleeding a lot.

• Machine nouns and verbs

5 Choose the correct option.

1 *Plug* / *Attach* the machine into the outlet.
2 *Attach* / *Press* the cord to the back of the machine.
3 *Produce* / *Press* the button to start the machine.
4 Do you know how energy is *communicated* / *produced*?
5 We usually *invent* / *communicate* by email or text.
6 You should always *plug in* / *turn off* machines when they aren't in use.

• Word building

6 Complete the text with the correct form of the words.

The [1] *inventors* (invent) of the first hot-air balloon were the Montgolfier brothers. They [2] .... (build) the balloon in 1793. The idea for the [3] .... (invent) came when they burned some paper. The fire [4] .... (product) hot air, which made the paper float up into the air. Later, they [5] .... (designer) a balloon from cloth and paper. They made a fire under it. The first passengers were a duck, a sheep and a chicken.

Word list

Unit 7 • Make a Difference

Protest and support

banner	/ˈbænɚ/
charity	/ˈtʃærəti/
collection	/kəˈlɛkʃən/
demonstration	/ˌdɛmənˈstreɪʃən/
donation	/doʊˈneɪʃən/
fundraising event	/ˈfʌndreɪzɪŋ ɪˌvɛnt/
march (n)	/mɑrtʃ/
petition (n)	/pəˈtɪʃən/
sign (n)	/saɪn/
sit-in (n)	/ˈsɪt ɪn/
slogan	/ˈsloʊgən/
volunteer (n)	/ˌvɑlənˈtɪr/

Verb + preposition

agree with	/əˈgri wɪð, wɪθ/
apologize for	/əˈpɑləˌdʒaɪz fɚ, fɔr/
argue with	/ˈɑrgyu wɪð, wɪθ/
believe in	/bəˈliv ɪn/
care about	/ˈkɛr əˌbaʊt/
decide on	/dɪˈsaɪd ɔn/
disapprove of	/ˌdɪsəˈpruv əv/
hope for	/ˈhoʊp fɚ, fɔr/
insist on	/ɪnˈsɪst ɔn, ɑn/
know about	/ˈnoʊ əˌbaʊt/
protest about	/ˈproʊtɛst əˌbaʊt/
worry about	/ˈwɚi, ˈwʌri əˌbaʊt/

Unit 8 • Danger and Risk

Extreme adjectives

awful	/ˈɔfəl/
burning	/ˈbɚnɪŋ/
excellent	/ˈɛksələnt/
exhausted	/ɪgˈzɔstɪd/
freezing	/ˈfrizɪŋ/
furious	/ˈfyʊriəs/
huge	/hyudʒ/
terrifying	/ˈtɛrəˌfaɪ-ɪŋ/
thrilled	/θrɪld/
tiny	/ˈtaɪni/

Illness and injury

a backache	/ˈbækeɪk/
a burn	/bɚn/
a cold	/koʊld/
a cough	/kɔf/
a cut	/kʌt/
a fever	/ˈfivɚ/
a headache	/ˈhedeɪk/
a rash	/ræʃ/
a sore throat	/ˌsɔr ˈθroʊt/
a sprained ankle	/ˌspreɪnd ˈæŋkəl/
a stomachache	/ˈstʌmək-eɪk/
a toothache	/ˈtuθeɪk/

Unit 9 • Inventions

Machine verbs

attach	/əˈtætʃ/
build	/bɪld/
communicate	/kəˈmyunəˌkeɪt/
invent	/ɪnˈvɛnt/
plug in	/ˌplʌg ˈɪn/
press	/prɛs/
produce	/prəˈdus/
turn off	/ˌtɚn ˈɔf/
turn on	/ˌtɚn ˈɔn/

Machine nouns

battery	/ˈbætəri/
button	/ˈbʌtn/
cable	/ˈkeɪbəl/
jack	/dʒæk/
keyboard	/ˈkibɔrd/
outlet	/ˈaʊtˀlɛt/
power cord	/ˌpaʊɚ ˈkɔrd/
remote control	/rɪˌmoʊt kənˈtroʊl/
tube	/tub/
wheel	/wil/

Word building

build	/bɪld/
builder	/ˈbɪldɚ/
building	/ˈbɪldɪŋ/
design	/dɪˈzaɪn/
designer	/dɪˈzaɪnɚ/
design	/dɪˈzaɪn/
invent	/ɪnˈvɛnt/
inventor	/ɪnˈvɛntɚ/
invention	/ɪnˈvɛnʃən/
paint	/peɪnt/
painter	/ˈpeɪntɚ/
painting	/ˈpeɪntɪŋ/
produce	/prəˈdus/
producer	/prəˈdusɚ/
product	/ˈprɑdʌkt/
write	/raɪt/
writer	/ˈraɪt̬ɚ/
writing	/ˈraɪt̬ɪŋ/

Brain Trainers

Unit 4

Find the difference

1 Look at the photo on page 48 for one minute. Now study this photo. What differences can you find?

Vocabulary

2 How many *news* words can you think of in one minute? Try to remember at least seven.

1 *local news*

3a Read the pairs of words aloud three times. Cover them and read the list below. Which word is missing?

quietly → loudly carefully → carelessly
happily → sadly patiently → angrily

carefully	angrily	loudly	happily
quietly	patiently	carelessly	

3b Now make more adverbs using the different colored letters. Then match the opposites.

well – badly

Unit 5

Find the difference

1 Look at the photo on page 8 for one minute. Now study this photo. What differences can you find?

Vocabulary

2 Look at the pictures for two minutes. Try to remember them in order. Then cover them. Take turns making suggestions. Can you remember all nine?

Brain Trainers

3a Find six meanings for the verb *get* in the puzzle. You have two minutes.

3b Think of one more meaning for the verb *get*.

b	g	h	s	p	n	r
b	r	i	n	g	r	e
e	a	b	m	i	d	c
c	l	u	o	c	r	e
o	h	y	v	y	k	i
m	u	r	e	n	e	v
e	a	r	r	i	v	e

Unit 6

Find the difference

1 Look at the photo on page 18 for one minute. Now study this photo. What differences can you find?

Vocabulary

2 Work in small groups. Choose an activity from the box. Act it out. Your classmates guess the activity.

do the dishes	feed the cat
set the table	mow the lawn
do the ironing	make the bed
cook a meal	do the laundry
wash the car	sweep the floor

3 Look at the faces carefully. Match them with the feelings adjectives. Write the answers in your notebook. Then check your answers on page 65.

relaxed	confused	nervous	upset
confident	disappointed	embarrassed	fed up

1 *fed up*

Brain Trainers

Unit 7

Find the difference

1 Look at the photo on page 32 for one minute. Now study this photo. What differences can you find?

Vocabulary

2 How many protest words and phrases can you think of with the letter *n* in them? Think of ten.

a banner

3 Read the phrases for two minutes. Cover the list and write the phrases in your notebook. How many can you remember?

care about	argue with
hope for	apologize for
decide on	worry about
disapprove of	agree with
know about	believe in
protest against	insist on

Unit 8

Find the difference

1 Look at the photo on page 42 for one minute. Now study this photo. What differences can you find?

Vocabulary

2 Look at the photos. Use an extreme adjective to describe each one. You have two minutes.

1 *huge*

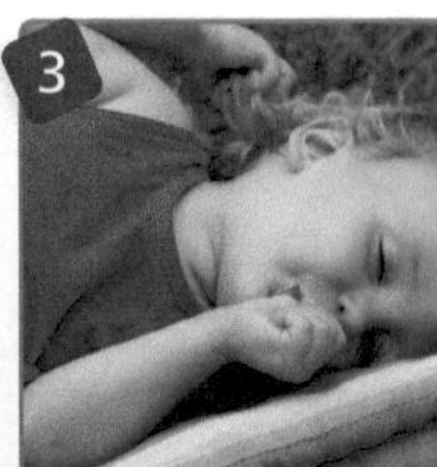

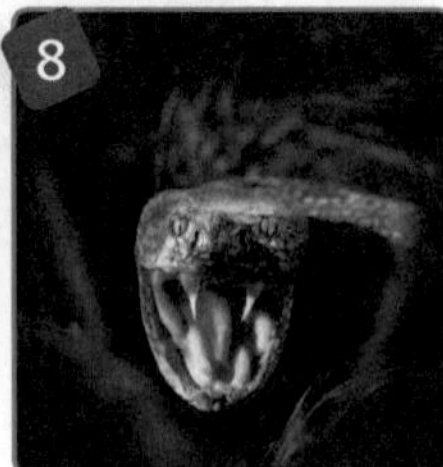

Which two extreme adjectives are missing?

Brain Trainers

3 Work in small groups. Choose an illness or injury. Act it out. Your classmates guess the problem.

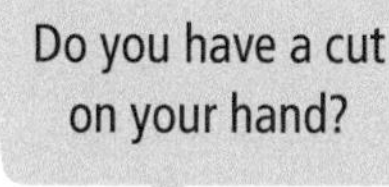

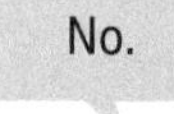

Do you have a burn?

Yes, I do!

Unit 9

Find the difference

1 Look at the photo on page 52 for one minute. Now study this photo. What differences can you find?

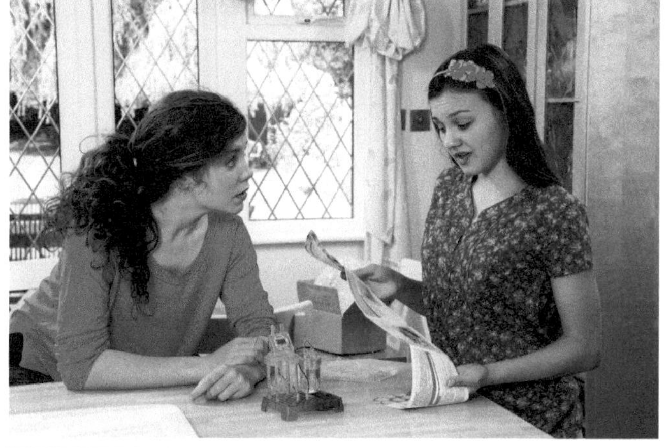

Vocabulary

2a Read the colored words and phrases aloud three times. Cover them and read the list below. Which word was missing?

cable button communicate
plug in press turn on keyboard

plug in	outlet	press	button
turn on	keyboard	cable	communicate

2b Now try again.

attach remote control tube
battery wheel invent build

invent	wheel	build	battery
attach	tube	turn off	remote control

3a Make words. Each word has three shapes.

in-ven-tor

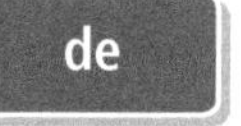

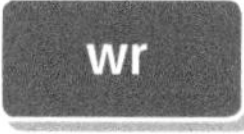

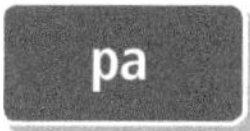

in	it	ner
de	il	ter
wr	ven	der
bu	in	er
pa	sig	tor

3b Now say what each person does. What is the result of their work?

An inventor ....

The result is ....

Listening Bank

Unit 5

1 **Listen. Choose the correct answers.**

2.22

1 Which country did Troy just visit?
   a *Fiji*
   b Japan
   c Turkey
2 What can you do in the first hotel?
   a open the windows
   b feed the fish
   c go swimming
3 What can you find in the second hotel?
   a an alarm clock
   b big windows
   c a large bed
4 What are rooms at the third hotel like?
   a dark and wet
   b warm and comfortable
   c very small
5 Which place does Troy recommend for a vacation?
   a Fiji
   b Japan
   c Turkey

2 **Listen again. Answer the questions.**

2.22

1 Where was the hotel in Fiji?
   25 meters under the sea
2 What does each room in the hotel have?
3 What's unusual about the hotel in Japan?
4 Are there any beds in the hotel?
5 Where is the hotel in Cappadocia?
6 Why does Troy recommend Cappadocia for a vacation?

Unit 6

1 **Listen again. Choose the correct options.**

2.35

Conversation 1

1 The boy thinks the girl should wear
   a pants. b shorts. c *a dress.*
2 The girl can't wear this because it's
   a not small enough. b too small. c horrible.

Conversation 2

3 The boy has to
   a clear the table.
   b hang out laundry.
   c set the table.
4 The boy is feeling
   a grateful. b glad. c fed up.

Conversation 3

5 The boy wants to go to a party with
   a robots. b football players. c his mom.
6 He can't go to the party because it's too
   a late. b expensive. c far away.

Conversation 4

7 The girl is having problems with
   a her English. b her computer. c her math.
8 The boy thinks she should
   a learn from him.
   b learn from his teacher.
   c become a teacher.

Cappadocia

Listening Bank

Unit 7

1 3.9 **Listen again. Complete the information pamphlet.**

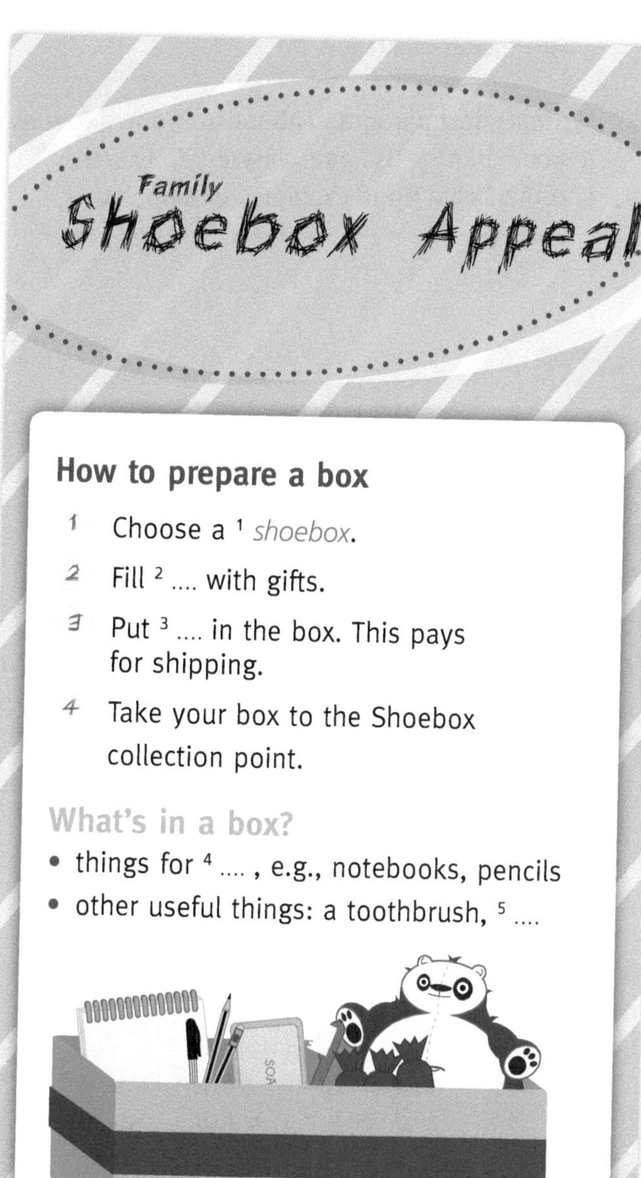

Family
Shoebox Appeal

How to prepare a box

1 Choose a [1] *shoebox*.
2 Fill [2] .... with gifts.
3 Put [3] .... in the box. This pays for shipping.
4 Take your box to the Shoebox collection point.

What's in a box?

- things for [4] .... , e.g., notebooks, pencils
- other useful things: a toothbrush, [5] ....

Don't put in

- medicine, [6] .... or scissors.

Unit 8

1 3.23 **Listen again. Choose the correct options to complete the advertisement.**

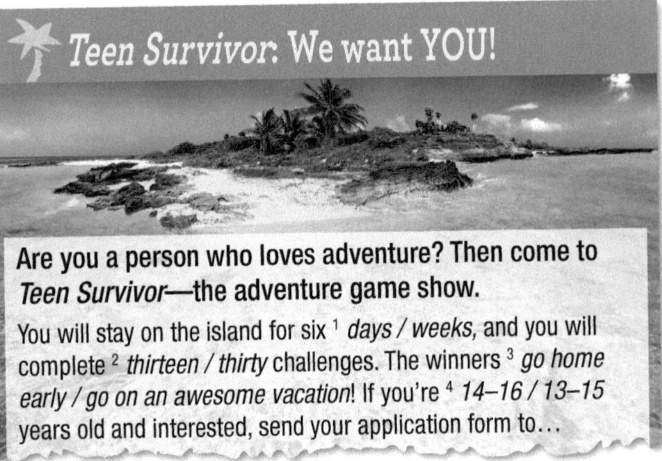

Teen Survivor: We want YOU!

Are you a person who loves adventure? Then come to *Teen Survivor*—the adventure game show.

You will stay on the island for six [1] *days / weeks*, and you will complete [2] *thirteen / thirty* challenges. The winners [3] *go home early / go on an awesome vacation*! If you're [4] *14–16 / 13–15* years old and interested, send your application form to…

2 3.23 **Listen again. Are these statements true (T) or false (F)?**

1 The girl saw an announcement in a magazine. *F*
2 The girl and boy both watch the show.
3 The show is on a desert island.
4 The boy is worried about the challenges.
5 The girl is interested in the prize.
6 They can both apply for the show.

Unit 9

1 3.36 **Listen to the conversation. What advantages and disadvantages of reading on a smart phone did the speakers mention?**

2 3.36 **Listen again. Are these statements true (T) or false (F)?**

1 The boy read a horror story on his smart phone. *F*
2 The boy reads at the bus stop.
3 He likes carrying books with him because they're small.
4 The girl thinks smart phone screens are a good size for reading.
5 The boy has thirteen e-books on his smart phone.
6 The girl likes keeping her books for years.

3 **Correct the false statements from Exercise 2.**

1 *The boy read a science fiction story on his smart phone.*

Culture 4 Robin Hood

Reading

1 (3.44) **Read about Robin Hood. Are these descriptions true (T), false (F) or don't know (DK)?**

a character in TV shows	a hero
a king	a real thief
the Sheriff of Nottingham	

2 **Read about Robin Hood again. Answer the questions.**

1 Why did Robin Hood go to the Middle East?
2 Why did he and his friends steal money?
3 How long have there been stories about Robin Hood?
4 Why do people visit the Major Oak?

Your Culture

3 **In pairs, answer the questions.**

1 What traditional heroes are there in your culture?
2 What do they do in the stories about them?
3 Are the stories true?

4 **Write a short paragraph about traditional heroes in your country. Use your answers to Exercise 3 and the Robin Hood examples to help you.**

Robin Hood

A statue of Robin Hood in Nottingham

The Major Oak

Robin Hood is England's most famous hero. What do we know about him?

The stories

Robin was a rich man from the north of England. He was very good at archery and went to the Middle East to fight with King Richard I. When he came home, the Sheriff of Nottingham took his lands, so he lived in Sherwood Forest with a group of friends—Little John, Will Scarlett and others. They stole money from the rich and gave it to the poor.

Are the stories true?

We don't know. There are a lot of old documents about the thieves at the end of the twelfth century, when Richard I was king. But no one has found documents about a Robin Hood in Nottingham.

Robin Hood today

Robin Hood has been the hero of songs and stories for more than six hundred years, and there have been more than fifty films and TV shows about him. There is a big Robin Hood celebration in Nottingham every year. People wear twelfth-century clothes, listen to stories and music and try archery. They also go to the Robin Hood Visitor Center in Sherwood Forest and see a big, old tree known as the Major Oak. In some stories, Robin hid from the Sheriff's men inside it.

Russell Crowe as Robin Hood in the 2010 movie

Culture  Multicultural America

Reading

1 3.45 **Read about Multicultural America. Match the different groups of people (1–4) to these things.**

Chinatown	civil rights	Hawaii
jazz	newspapers	two percent

2 Read about Multicultural America again. Complete the sentences.

1 Five percent of the people in the US are .... .
2 You can buy Spanish .... and hear Spanish radio in American cities.
3 African Americans fought for .... and .... rights throughout American history.
4 People with parents from different ethnic groups are called .... .

Your Culture

3 In pairs, answer the questions.

1 What ethnic groups are there in your country?
2 How long have they lived there?
3 What other countries' food is popular in your country?
4 Are there many immigrants in your country? Where do many people emigrate from?

4 Write a short paragraph about different cultures in your country. Use your answers to Exercise 3 and the Multicultural America examples to help you.

Multicultural America

Many groups of people have come to the land inhabited by Native American tribes, now known as the United States of America. The following are some important racial and ethnic groups in the United States.

1 African American

Africans were brought to North America as slaves by Europeans when the land was colonized by the British and the French in the seventeenth century. African Americans now make up 13 percent of the population. Many of the best-known aspects of American culture, such as jazz, rock and hip hop music, come from African American culture. The African Americans' fight for freedom and civil rights has defined American history.

2 Hispanic or Latino

The land that is now Texas, California and the American Southwest belonged to Mexico until the mid-nineteenth century. People from all the Central and South American countries continue to migrate to the United States, increasing the Latino community. Overall, 17 percent of the US population is Hispanic. Latinos are also the fastest-growing group. Spanish is the second most commonly spoken language in the US after English, and Spanish-language newspapers, radio stations and TV channels are widely available. Food from Latin American countries, especially Mexico, is also very popular in the US.

3 Asian and Pacific Islander

Asians (including South Asians) and native Hawaiians, along with other Pacific Islanders, make up 5 percent of the US population, with significant communities on both the East and West Coasts. Every major city has its "Chinatown," a predominantly Asian neighborhood. The two most famous Chinatowns are in San Francisco and New York City. People in the US enjoy Asian and South Asian foods, especially Chinese, Japanese and Indian food.

4 Mixed race

Two percent of American children are mixed race—their parents come from different ethnic groups.

Culture 6 Canada

Reading

1 3.46 **Read about Canada. What is the most important language in each region?**

1 Ontario
2 Quebec
3 Nunavut

2 Read about Canada again. Complete the sentences with place names.

1 The capital city of Canada is .... .
2 Niagara Falls is a popular place for visitors in the .... region.
3 A lot of maple syrup comes from .... .
4 People in the town of .... don't see the sun for four months in winter.

Your Culture

3 In pairs, answer the questions.

1 What are the most popular places in your country for visitors from other countries?
2 Are there regions in your country where the country's official language isn't the principal language? Do people in these regions want to be independent? Give examples.
3 What food is your country or region famous for?
4 Are there any regions where few people live? Why don't more people live there?

4 Write a short paragraph about different regions in your country. Use your answers to Exercise 3 and the Canada examples to help you.

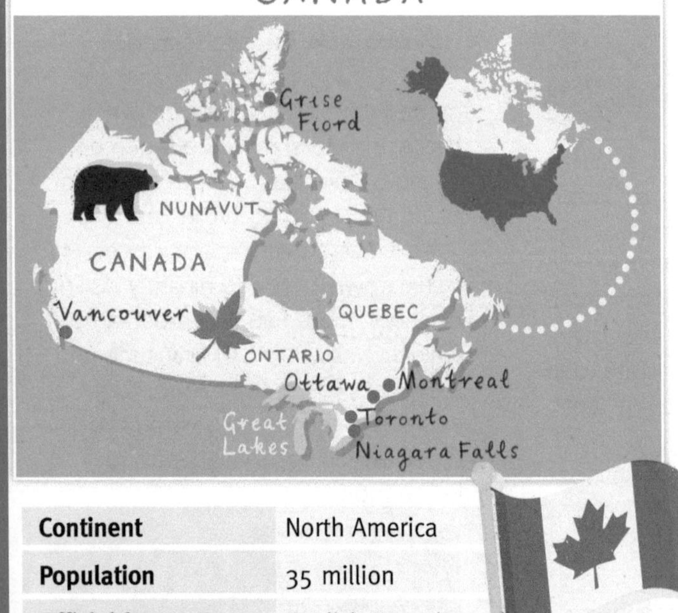

Continent	North America
Population	35 million
Official languages	English, French
Currency	Canadian dollar
Favorite sport	Ice hockey

Canada is the world's second-largest country, but a lot of the land in the center and north is uninhabited. Canada is famous for its cold winters and beautiful mountains.

Ontario
Canada's biggest city, Toronto, and its capital, Ottawa, are in this region. Here, as in most of Canada, English is the principal language. A lot of people come here to visit Niagara Falls and the Great Lakes.

Quebec
Canada's second-biggest city, Montreal, is here. Most people in Quebec speak French, and about 40 percent want Quebec to be an independent country. The majority of Canada's maple syrup comes from Quebec. Canadians eat this delicious syrup with pancakes, and the leaf of the maple tree even appears on their flag.

Nunavut
Nunavut is the biggest region in Canada, yet only 33,000 people live there. There are no trees, and the land and sea are frozen for most of the year. It is easier to travel by snowmobile than by car. At Grise Fiord, the farthest north of Nunavut's towns, people endure four months without daylight in winter and four months without night in summer. Most people in Nunavut are Inuit. They speak the Inuit language, but they don't live in igloos. They have houses with TVs and Internet.

MOVE IT!

WORKBOOK WITH MP3S

JOE MCKENNA
SERIES CONSULTANT: CARA NORRIS-RAMIREZ

Contents

5 Enjoy Your Vacation! 74

6 That's Life! 82

Check 2 90

7 Make a Difference 92

8 Danger and Risk 100

9 Inventions 108

Check 3 116

Language Reference and Practice

Grammar Reference 118

Vocabulary 128

Speaking and Listening 133

Pronunciation 138

Irregular Verb List 140

My Assessment Profile 141

5 Enjoy Your Vacation!

Vocabulary • Vacation

★ **1 Match the sentence beginnings (1–7) to the endings (a–g).**

1 Do you eat out on vacation, *e*
2 I prefer to stay in hotels,
3 We like to go camping
4 I've only seen a few sights
5 Do you often take trips
6 We got lost in the city
7 She's written a travel blog

a or do you prefer to vacation at home?
b and we don't mind what the weather's like.
c and had to take a taxi back.
d about her trip to Turkey.
e or do you cook in the apartment?
f because many of them are closed.
g but I can't usually afford to.

★★ **2 Complete the sentences with the correct form of these verbs.**

book	buy	check into	get
~~lose~~	pack	put up	

1 Good morning! Unfortunately, they've *lost* our luggage!
2 The weather was cold and cloudy, so he didn't .... a tan.
3 Dad, you should learn how to .... a tent before going on vacation!
4 Have you .... your bags for the trip?
5 Our neighbors have .... a two-week hotel stay in Portugal.
6 We .... the hotel and then went out for a walk.
7 How many souvenirs have you .... ?

★★ **3 Choose the correct options.**

1 Jorge and Maria *went* / *booked* a resort in the Caribbean.
2 They didn't usually *take* / *go* a trip, but this year was different.
3 They *put up* / *packed* their bags at home.
4 They had a good flight, but they *got lost* / *lost* their luggage.
5 So they didn't *go* / *get* sightseeing when they arrived.
6 Instead of *staying* / *buying* souvenirs, they had to *stay* / *buy* clothes!

★★ **4 Complete the conversation with these words**

hotel	hotel	luggage	sightseeing
~~souvenirs~~	tan	tent	

A So what was Miami like?
B Wonderful!
A Did you buy any [1] *souvenirs*?
B Just a few things for the family.
A Did you book the [2]........................ , or did you look for a room when you arrived?
B We went without a hotel reservation. The idea was to go camping, but there was no place to put up a [3]........................ .
A What about the campgrounds?
B They were too crowded.
A So what did you do?
B We checked into a cheap [4]........................ and stayed there.
A Did you go [5]........................ ?
B Not really! We just went to the beach and got a good [6]........................ .
A Yes, I noticed! So you had a good time?
B Yes, except that Derek lost his [7]........................ on the way home!
A What a shame!

Workbook page 128

Reading

★ **1 Read the texts quickly and choose the best title.**

a Your Adventure Vacation
b Your Cheap Vacation
c Your Family Vacation

Madison

In my family, we've been to the beach every summer since I was little. It's always been fun because we live in a big city and the change is great! I love staying in a hotel because I don't have to make the bed, and we love eating out because my parents don't have to cook, and I don't have to do the dishes afterward! And we all enjoy getting a good tan. But the best of all is that my parents pay for the vacation!

Noah

There are six of us in our family, so we've often had problems with vacations. But for the last five years, we've agreed together on where we want to go. Last year we booked a flight to Chicago. Then when we got there, we decided to have time to go sightseeing in the city, time to go shopping for souvenirs and then free time for different activities. That way, we avoid a lot of silly arguments!

We're twin brothers, and we've gone on a lot of different vacations with our parents. We've usually enjoyed them too, except for museums and monuments, which are a little boring. So this year, because we're already 16, our parents let us go camping with some friends, and it was awesome. We did a lot of walking and climbing, we didn't get lost, and it wasn't expensive.

Rob and Doug

★ **2 Complete the sentences with the correct names.**

1 *Noah* flew to Chicago last year.
2 .... had a new kind of vacation this year.
3 .... usually goes to the beach.
4 .... didn't go with the family this year.
5 .... often goes to a hotel.
6 ....'s family organizes the way they spend their time.

★★ **3 Are the statements true (T) or false (F)?**

1 Madison lives in a small town. *F*
2 She often does chores at home. ....
3 Noah's family can't always agree on what to do. ....
4 They had a lot of arguments last year. ....
5 The twins aren't very interested in museums and monuments. ....
6 They had a pretty lazy vacation this year. ....

Brain Trainer 

Underline these adjectives in the texts in Exercise 1:

boring
silly
expensive
free
awesome
different

Now do Exercise 1.

Grammar • Present perfect + *for* and *since*; *How long?*

★ **1 Choose the correct options.**

1 We've been here (for) / *since* six days.
2 She's read three books *for / since* we arrived.
3 They haven't been camping *for / since* 2012.
4 We haven't watched TV *for / since* a week!
5 I haven't stayed in a hotel *for / since* I was ten!
6 They haven't stopped dancing *for / since* three hours!

★ **2 Rewrite the sentences. Put *for* or *since* in the correct place.**

1 My family has lived here ten years.
My family has lived here for ten years.
2 I've gone to this school 2012.
....
3 Carrie and I have been friends we were kids.
....
4 We haven't seen Grandma a long time.
....
5 I've wanted a new bicycle six months.
....

★★ **3 Complete the conversation with these words.**

the end of	the last five weeks	the last two
last weekend	three years	~~your birthday~~

A Irene! I haven't seen you since [1] *your birthday* in May! How are you?
B Fine, thanks! And you? Where have you been for [2] .... months?
A Oh, I've been traveling, you know. I had an exchange trip to Mexico. I've only been home since [3] ....
B Did you have a good time?
A It was very interesting, yes. I've studied Spanish for [4] .... now, so I was able to practice a lot! But what about you? What's new?
B I've been on vacation since [5] .... June, when school finished. And I've had a summer job for [6] .... , so I'm earning a little money.
A That's wonderful! I'm very happy for you!

★★ **4 Write sentences to complete the postcard.**

POSTCA

Hi Jackie!
Here we are in Italy! [1] *We / be here / ten days*, and it's been great. [2] *We / go / beach / every day / we arrived*, and the water's perfect. [3] *My parents / rent a car / five days*, so we're doing some sightseeing as well. I'm writing now from Venice. [4] *We / be / in the city / ten o'clock this morning*, and there are more tourists than local people! We're having a drink in a café, and [5] *I / write / five postcards / we sat down at the table.* I wanted to write a travel blog, of course, but [6] *I / be / too busy / our vacation started*, so you'll have to wait until we get back home before you see the photos. Our vacation has been a little tiring, but [7] *I / sleep / very well / we got here!*
Love,
Lucas

1 *We've been here for ten days.*
2 ....
3 ....
4 ....
5 ....
6 ....
7 ....

★ **5 Make questions for the underlined answers.**

1 I've sent <u>twenty</u> text messages since this morning.
2 She's had her MP3 player <u>since Christmas</u>.
3 He's been on the plane <u>for four hours</u>.
4 They've driven <u>three hundred</u> kilometers today.
5 She hasn't gotten up early <u>for a week</u>!
6 We've been at the beach <u>since two o'clock</u>.

1 *How many text messages have you sent?*
2 ....
3 ....
4 ....
5 ....
6 ....

Grammar Reference pages 118–119

Vocabulary • Meanings of *get*

★ **1** **Match these verbs to the meanings of *get* in the sentences (1–6). Use the correct forms.**

arrive	buy	~~bring~~	become	receive	walk

1 Can you get me some milk from the fridge?
bring
2 I got this new shirt on sale.
....
3 What time did you get home after the party?
....
4 We got on the bus near the stadium.
....
5 When it got dark, we made a fire.
....
6 Did you get that watch for your birthday?
....

★ **2** **Choose the correct meaning for the verb *get*.**

1 I got a phone call from my friend.
brought / (received)
2 We got off the bus across the street from the station.
arrived at / walked
3 We got to the hotel about three o'clock.
bought / arrived at
4 It got cold in the room.
became / brought
5 Room service got some blankets for us.
brought / bought
6 We got some souvenirs the next morning.
bought / became

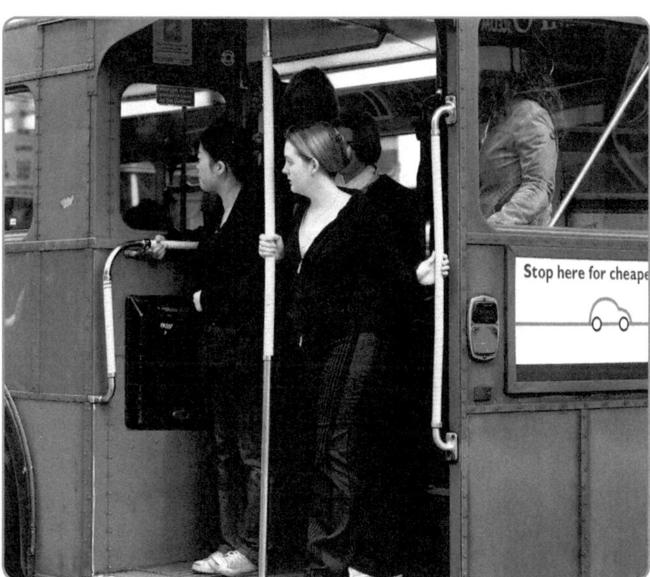

★ **3** **Put the words in the correct order.**

1 **A** this / school / you / get / did / to / morning / How / ?
How did you get to school this morning?
B I took the bus.
2 **A** Why did you switch on the light?
B frightened / the / Because / I / in / got / dark
....
3 **A** Have you seen my jacket anywhere?
B you / moment / Yes, / it / for / in / I'll / a / get
....
4 **A** Did you have a good time at the market?
B new / some / Yes, / I / shoes / got
....
5 **A** What happened to your friend?
B train / He / the / got / disappeared / on / and / !
....
6 **A** message / Did / my / get / you / ?
....
B What message? I haven't seen any messages!

★★ **4** **Read the text. Replace *get* with the correct form of these verbs.**

arrive at	become	buy	bring	receive	~~walk~~

We [1] **got** off the train at a small station in the countryside, and walked to the campground. It [2] **was getting** dark, and we were tired from the trip. When we [3] **got to** the campsite, it was difficult to see. We had to [4] **get** a flashlight from the man in the small corner store at the entrance, and then we went to put up the tent. Half an hour later, we were still trying, but we were lucky because we [5] **got** some help from one of the other campers. Then we sent Joe to [6] **get** some wood, so we could light a fire.

1 *walked*
2 ....
3 ....
4 ....
5 ....
6 ....

Workbook page 128

Chatroom Asking for information

Speaking and Listening

★ **1** 20 **Match the questions (1–6) to the answers (a–f). Then listen and check.**

1 Excuse me! Can you help us? *f*
2 Where's a good place to buy souvenirs?
3 Is there a good place to have coffee there?
4 How can we get there?
5 Is it far?
6 How long does it take to get to the bus station?

a It's about a ten-minute walk.
b Yes, there's a nice little café on the corner.
c Not really. It's less than one kilometer.
d There's a good store across from the museum.
e Well, you can walk or take a bus.
f Sure! What are you looking for?

★ **2** 21 **Put the conversation in the correct order. Then listen and check.**

a Is it far from here? ....
b Oh, yes! That's next to the church on North Street. ....
c Thanks very much! ....
d Excuse me! Can you help me? *1*
e It's about five minutes down that street over there. ....
f Sure! What's the problem? ....
g I'm looking for a restaurant called Cool Kitchen. ....

★★ **3** 22 **Complete the conversation with these words. Then listen and check.**

~~a good place~~	can I get	go down this street
How long	on the left	the mall

A Excuse me! Can you help me?
B Sure! What do you need?
A Is there [1] *a good place* to buy camera batteries near here?
B There's a camera store on Main Street, but that's a little far away from here.
A [2]........................ does it take to get there?
B It takes a while if you're walking.
A How about a big grocery store? They usually have batteries.
B OK! Yes, there's one next to [3]........................ down the street.
A How [4]........................ there?
B It's about a ten-minute walk.
A Great!
B OK. Well, [5]........................ till you see a big church on the corner.
A All right.
B Then cross the intersection [6]........................ , and the mall's on the other side of the street.
A Perfect! Thanks very much.
B You're welcome!

★★ **4** 22 **Listen to the conversation in Exercise 3 again. Choose the correct options.**

1 There are (*two*) / *three* places to buy camera batteries.
2 Main Street *is* / *isn't* near where the speakers are.
3 The camera store *is* / *isn't* in the mall.
4 The girl *is visiting* / *lives in* the town.
5 The mall is *before* / *after* the intersection.

★★ **5** **Write a conversation. Use phrases from Exercises 1–3 and this information:**

An English-speaking tourist in your hometown asks you about a good place to eat out. You recommend a restaurant and describe its location.

Speaking and Listening page 133

Grammar • Past simple with *just*

★ **1 Match the questions (1–6) to the answers (a–f).**

1 What's the matter with Derek? *c*
2 Has anyone seen my glasses?
3 Is this the bus for Providence?
4 Did I give you my cell phone?
5 Are those my class notes?
6 Can I speak to Felicity, please?

a Sorry! I just spilled water on them!
b Sorry, she just went out.
c He just lost his luggage.
d I'm sorry, you just missed it.
e You just sat on them, Grandma.
f No! You just put it in your bag!

★ **2 Complete the sentences with the correct form of these verbs.**

blow	go	lose	melt	put	~~use~~

1 Somebody just *used* all the sunscreen!
2 I just .... my hotel key card.
3 The wind just .... my magazine into the pool!
4 We bought ice cream, but it just .... !
5 Lewis just .... up the tent, and there's a coyote coming this way!
6 I just .... shopping and forgot the eggs.

★ **3 Put the words in the correct order.**

1 travel / blog / just / London / about / I / wrote / a
I just wrote a travel blog about London.
2 prize / in / just / a / Liz / a / competition / won
....
3 bought / new / dad / just / Jake's / a / car
....
4 booked / a / Shane / hotel / just / Germany / in
....
5 Colorado / They / came / camping / back / from / in / just
....
6 ate / good / just / restaurant / a / very / out / at / We
....

★★ **4 Look at the pictures. Write sentences using *just*.**

1 *He just fell off his bike.*
2 ....
3 ....
4 ....
5 ....
6 ....

Grammar Reference pages 118–119

Reading

1 **Read the text quickly. What kind of text is it?**

a a magazine article
b a travel blog
c a letter to someone's family

WEDNESDAY

We're continuing our week in Amsterdam. Mom and Dad have gone to the Rijksmuseum, and we just returned to the hotel from the Van Gogh Museum. It was modern and interesting. I liked the painting of his shoes, but Clara says the picture of the yellow house is her favorite. We also went to a huge street market where we bought some souvenirs.

THURSDAY

We've been up since seven o'clock this morning because we've been on a day trip to visit a real windmill. It was made of wood and was really pretty on the outside, but full of spiders' webs on the inside. It was really old, but it still worked! We had lunch in a little town before coming back to the city. (Did you know the Dutch have mayonnaise with their French fries?!)

And this afternoon we went for a walk in one of the big parks. I've never seen so many flowers!

FRIDAY

Tomorrow's our last day here. This morning we went to see Anne Frank's house, because I read the book in school last year, and I wanted to see it for myself. It made me think about how lucky I am. Anyway, we're eating out tonight at an Indonesian restaurant, so tomorrow's blog post will be about exotic food!

2 **Choose the correct options.**

1 The writer *visited* / *didn't visit* the Rijksmuseum.
2 They went shopping on *Wednesday* / *Thursday*.
3 The windmill *was* / *wasn't* very clean inside.
4 On Thursday afternoon, they *left* / *stayed in* the hotel.
5 To the writer, Anne Frank's house was *boring* / *interesting*.

Listening

1 23 **Listen and choose the correct options.**

1 The speaker is going to have *Chinese* / *Indian* / *Italian* food.
2 He and his friend have eaten a lot of *fast food* / *pizza* / *sandwiches* this week.
3 The woman says lunch at the restaurant costs *$6* / *$15* / *$16*.
4 The restaurant is *takeout* / *self-service* / *waiter service*.
5 The woman *explains how to get there* / *shows them the way on a map* / *takes them there herself*.

2 23 **Who says these phrases? Listen again and write B for the boy or W for the woman.**

1 What kind of food *W*
2 every day this week ....
3 I've eaten there ....
4 what's a buffet lunch? ....
5 you get the food yourself ....
6 Come with me! ....

Writing • A travel guide

1 **Complete the text with these adjectives.**

beautiful	helpful	~~historic~~
musical	popular	sunny

One of my favorite vacation places is the [1] *historic* city of Williamsburg in eastern Virginia. It's not too big, it has a lot of good stores and restaurants, and the people are friendly and [2]........................ . Spring is the best time to visit, when the weather's bright and [3]........................ , and the flowers are in bloom. There are a lot of things to see and do in and around Williamsburg. The Revolutionary City is the most famous and [4]........................ attraction. You can visit all of it, and it's interactive: you can see people wearing eighteenth-century clothes, hear the [5].................... instruments and smell the spices they cooked with. You can even meet the heroes of the American Revolution, like Thomas Jefferson, George Washington and Patrick Henry! And there are [6]........................ eighteenth-century gardens you can tour. For day trips, you can go to an adventure park, visit Jamestown—the first permanent English settlement in America—go fishing in the river, play golf and other sports, or watch the race cars in nearby Richmond. Williamsburg is easy to get to by car, bus or train. Check it out on the Internet!

2 **Complete the chart with adjectives from the text. Then write more adjectives you remember.**

places	*historic*
people	
weather	
tourist attractions	

3 **Complete column A with ideas from the text in Exercise 1.**

	A Williamsburg	B My favorite vacation destination: ....
Introduction: Where is it? What are the people like? When is the best time to visit and why?	*Eastern Virginia*	
What is there to see and do?		
Conclusion: How can you get there? Where can you get more information?		

4 **Add ideas for your own favorite vacation destination to column B.**

5 **Write a travel guide in three paragraphs. Use your ideas and the adjectives and phrases from Exercises 2, 3 and 4.**

....
....
....
....
....
....
....
....
....
....
....
....

6 That's Life!

Vocabulary • Household chores

★ **1 Match the verbs (1–8) to the nouns (a–h).**

1 clear	a the floor
2 do	b the trash
3 feed	c the laundry
4 sweep	d the car
5 make	e the table
6 hang out	f the cat
7 take out	g the ironing
8 wash	h your bed

★★ **2 Complete the sentences with the correct form of these verbs.**

cook	do	wash	set
load	mow	vacuum	~~walk~~

1 Who's going to *walk* the dog this afternoon?
2 It's raining! Did you .... the car this morning?
3 You .... the dishwasher, but you didn't turn it on!
4 Is it your turn to .... lunch?
5 You need to .... the lawn today!
6 Could you .... the table for six, please?
7 I .... the dishes yesterday!
8 Have you .... the carpet yet?

★★ **3 Choose the correct options.**

1 Breakfast is finished! We need someone to *set* / *clear* the table!
2 Jonathan! Have you *made* / *done* your bed yet?
3 No brooms, please! It's much better to *sweep* / *vacuum* the floor.
4 The clothes are washed. You can *run* / *hang out* the laundry now!
5 Here's the clean laundry. Whose turn is it to *make* / *do* the ironing?
6 Mom! Don't leave without *setting* / *loading* the dishwasher!
7 Angela! I need you to *do* / *take out* the trash, please!

★★ **4 Use the information in the chart to write complete sentences.**

George's chore list

1 ✓	2 ✗
3 ✓	4 ✗
5 ✓	6 ✗
7 ✓	8 ✗

1 *George has cleared the table.*
2 ....
3 ....
4 ....
5 ....
6 ....
7 ....
8 ....

Workbook page 129

Reading

★ 1 **Match the names (1–3) to the number of people in their families (a–c).**

1 Becca	a four
2 Malcolm	b seven
3 Richie	c two

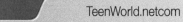

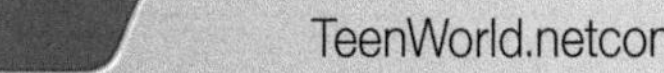

Teens and Chores

On the subject of teenagers and household chores, we asked: What happens in your home? Here are some of the answers you sent us.

Becca

I don't have to do very much at home because we have a housecleaner who does most of the chores. But my mom says I must learn some things, so I make my own bed every day. She also says I must take care of my pets, so I feed the cat and walk the dog in the afternoon. But I don't have to do the dishes or anything because that's what dishwashers are for!

Malcolm

My sister and I have to help with the chores. My parents have a chart on the fridge door, and every week we switch activities. This week I must load and unload the dishwasher, and my sister has to set and clear the table. But she's five years younger than me, so I often have to do more than her. She never has to mow the lawn, for example, or do the ironing.

Richie

There are five children in our family, and our parents tell us we must do our share of the housework. The older children have to do things like cook meals and take out the trash. The younger ones have to do smaller chores, like clear the table and load the dishwasher.

★ 2 **Choose the correct options.**

1 *Becca* / *Malcolm* does a lot of chores.
2 *Malcolm* / *Richie* does more than his younger sister.
3 *Becca* / *Richie* has to take care of animals.
4 Only members of the family do the chores in *Becca's* / *Malcolm's* home.
5 The younger children usually do the easier chores in *Richie's* / *Becca's* home.

★★ 3 **Complete the sentences.**

1 Becca has to do *some* chores every day.
2 Becca doesn't have to do the …………………… .
3 Malcolm can see his chores on the …………………… .
4 Malcolm's sister doesn't have to do …………………… chores.
5 Richie gives …………………… examples of the chores for the children in his home.

Grammar • Have to/Don't have to • Must/Mustn't

★ 1 **Read the chart. Are the statements true (T) or false (F)?**

	Millie	Mark
make the bed	✓	✓
do the ironing	✗	✓
do the laundry	✗	✗
cook a meal	✓	✓
walk the dog	✓	✗
mow the lawn	✗	✗
wash the car	✗	✓

1 Millie has to do more chores than Mark. *F*
2 Millie and Mark have to make the bed. ....
3 Only Millie has to do the ironing. ....
4 Mark doesn't have to do the laundry. ....
5 Millie doesn't have to cook a meal. ....
6 Mark has to walk the dog. ....
7 Millie and Mark don't have to mow the lawn. ....

★★ 2 **Complete the questions with the correct form of the verbs. Add the correct verb in the answers.**

1 *Do you have to* (you/have to) clear the table? No, I *don't*.
2 .... (your brother/have to) sweep the floor? Yes, he ....
3 .... (your parents/have to) share the chores? Yes, they ....
4 .... (your sister/have to) take out the trash? No, she ....

★★ 3 **Complete the conversation with the correct form of *have to/don't have to*.**

A What kind of chores [1] *do you have to* (you) do at summer camp?
B I [2]...................... make my bed every morning.
A And outside your room? [3]...................... (you) work in the kitchen?
B No, I don't. The kitchen staff [4]...................... load and unload the dishwasher, and they also [5]...................... take the trash out.
A What about your clothes?
B We [6]...................... do the laundry because the supervisors do that, but we [7]...................... sweep the floor.

★ 4 **Read the sentences. Write O for Obligation, N/O for No obligation or P for Prohibition.**

1 You must do the dishes after breakfast! *O*
2 We mustn't feed the cat more than once a day. ....
3 I must make the bed before I go to school. ....
4 We don't have to cook any meals on weekdays. ....
5 My brother must walk the dog every morning. ....
6 Joanna doesn't have to do the ironing every day. ....
7 You mustn't wash the car in the street. ....

★★ 5 **Look at the rules for students sharing an apartment. Write sentences with *must/mustn't* and *have to/don't have to*.**

Students' rules

1 take out the trash before six o'clock P
2 do the laundry in the morning O
3 hang out the laundry on the balcony P
4 do the ironing in the kitchen N/O
5 vacuum the floor at night P
6 sweep the floor on the landing O
7 feed the neighbor's cats N/O

1 *We mustn't take out the trash before six o'clock.*
2 ....
3 ....
4 ....
5 ....
6 ....
7 ....

Grammar Reference pages 120–121

Vocabulary • Feelings adjectives

★ 1 **Complete the definitions with these adjectives.**

confident confused embarrassed fed up ~~grateful~~ guilty

1 When someone has solved a problem for you, you feel *grateful*.
2 When you do something wrong and don't admit it, you feel ....
3 When you make a big mistake in front of other people, you feel ....
4 When you know for sure that you can do something well, you feel ....
5 When you don't know what to do and can't make a decision, you feel ....
6 When other people do nothing and you have to do everything, you feel ....

★ 2 **Put the letters in the correct order to complete the text.**

FEBRUARY 24

Tuesday

Another day of ups and downs! Evan appeared today with a new smart phone, which is much better than mine—I felt so [1] *jealous* (asleujo)! And I got my math test grade: 65. I was a little [2] .... (depositpinda) because I studied a lot and I expected a higher score. But Stella got an 80, which is awesome, so I felt really [3] .... (dalg) for her. She was very [4] .... (rovenus) the day before the exam because her parents promised her some concert tickets if she passed. So she's been happy and [5] .... (eladrex) all day! Then in the library this afternoon, I was feeling kind of [6] .... (yellon) because Toby wasn't there. Stella said he was in trouble because she saw him outside the principal's office, so I got worried. But then Toby appeared. It was only a message, so I felt [7] .... (liedreve) that there was nothing wrong.

★★ 3 **Choose the correct options.**

1 Our team has won the last three games, so they're *confused* / *confident* about winning tomorrow.
2 I'm *fed up* / *nervous* with waiting for the bus. I think I'll just walk instead!
3 Janet got very *guilty* / *upset* the other day when she lost her cell phone.
4 Reggie is a little *jealous* / *confused* because my bike has better brakes than his.
5 I fell down in class and everyone laughed! I felt really *disappointed* / *embarrassed*.
6 I lost my address book on the weekend, but Sadie found it, so I felt *relieved* / *relaxed*.

★★ 4 **Complete the conversation with these words.**

~~confused~~ embarrassed fed up grateful lonely relaxed upset

A Did you see the TV show last night? The one about the friends who share an apartment?
B Yes, but I got a little [1] *confused* because the story wasn't very clear. Who was the boy that got [2] .... because someone spilled coffee on his laptop?
A That was Adam. In general, he's [3] .... with his roommates because he's neat and organized, and they're not! Their way of doing things is much more [4] ....
B You mean careless! So who was the girl whose face went so red?
A That was Nikki. She was [5] .... because she got Thierry's name wrong, and the others laughed. And that's why she was so [6] .... to Lucas for helping her.
B OK, now I understand better. Do you watch it regularly?
A Whenever I'm feeling a little [7] .... , I watch another episode. It's great!
B Cool!

Workbook page 129

Chatroom Giving advice

Speaking and Listening

★ 1 **Match the problems (1–6) to the advice (a–f). Then listen and check.**
24

1 I've been a little lonely recently. *d*
2 I'm tired of the same cereals!
3 I spend too much time on the Internet.
4 I miss my brother who's in Japan.
5 I don't get the presents I want.
6 I have to clean my room every week.

a I don't think you should complain. It only takes ten minutes!
b Maybe you should buy them yourself!
c Why don't you video call him?
d Maybe you should call your friends!
e Why don't you have toast, then?
f I think you should do more outdoor activities.

★ 2 **Put the words in the correct order to make answers. Then listen and check.**
25

1 **A** I'm not sure this T-shirt fits me very well.
B size / try / you / Why / different / a / don't / ?
Why don't you try a different size?

2 **A** I'd like to learn how to draw well.
B drawing / you / classes / take / Maybe / should
....

3 **A** I'm thinking about changing the color of my hair.
B that / I / worry / don't / you / should / think / about / !
....

4 **A** I want to eat more healthily.
B shouldn't / meals / Maybe / have / snacks / between / you / !
....

5 **A** I need a larger allowance.
B chores / you / home / should / do / think / more / at / I / first / !
....

6 **A** There's no room in my closet for all my clothes!
B new / I / should / many / think / clothes / don't / buy / so / you
....

★★ 3 **Complete the conversation with these words. Then listen and check.**
26

~~fed up~~	I don't think	I feel tired
Why don't you	you don't have time	You should

A You look [1] *fed up*! What's the matter?
B I have to get up very early for school, so [2]........................ all the time.
A Well, [3]........................ you should go to bed so late!
B And I hate having to wear the school uniform. Why can't I wear my own clothes?
A [4]........................ think about more important things?
B Like what?
A Like helping me with the chores! When you're busy working, [5]........................ to worry about anything else.
B Yes, but I have to study. And I get good grades at school!
A So you have nothing to worry about. [6]........................ learn to wake up with a smile!

★★ 4 **Listen to the conversation in Exercise 3 again. Complete the sentences with one word.**
26

1 Speaker B always feels *tired.*
2 Speaker B doesn't like .... a uniform.
3 Speaker A's opinions are .... from Speaker B's opinions.
4 Speaker A says it's more important to .... things than to worry.
5 Speaker A says that B should .... to be more positive in the morning.

★★ 5 **Write a conversation. Use expressions from Exercises 1–3, and this information:**

A friend tells you about a problem. Give your friend advice. Mention two things you think he/she should do and two things you think he/she shouldn't do.

Speaking and Listening page 134

Grammar • Predictions with *will, won't, might*

★ 1 **Choose the correct options.**

1 I don't think our visitors (will) / *might* arrive on time.
2 They're not sure about the weather. They *will* / *might* stay home instead.
3 She's a big Justin Bieber fan! She *will* / *might* go to the Bieber concert!
4 He doesn't read. He *won't* / *might not* pass his literature exam.
5 We haven't decided. We *will* / *might* go to visit Elaine's family.
6 School is closed today. There *won't* / *might not* be anyone in the office.
7 Shane's a little confused. He *will* / *might* study to be a mechanic.

★ 2 **Match the questions (1–6) to the answers (a–f).**

1 Do you think our team will win? *e*
2 Do you think she'll come to the party?
3 Do you think it will rain tomorrow?
4 Will John like his present?
5 Will Emma be glad to see me?
6 Will we get to the station in time?

a I know she will!
b With this traffic, I don't think we will.
c I don't know! He might not.
d She might, but she's working late today.
e I'm sure they will.
f I don't think it will. It's too sunny.

★★ 3 **Complete the sentences with *will, won't* or *might*.**

1 Uncle Tom's in China, so he *won't* be here tomorrow.
2 The hotel's next to a park, so it .... be very quiet.
3 The flight is on time, so Dad .... arrive in ten minutes.
4 I don't know what time they close, so they .... still be open.
5 The trains are very busy today, so you .... not get a ticket.
6 He's tired and nervous, so he .... be very happy if you make noise.

★★ 4 **Make sentences.**

1 our team / not win / because / not practice / hard enough. (won't)
Our team won't win because they haven't practiced hard enough.
2 Lennie / come / because / miss / bus. (won't)
....
....
3 Jack / not want / talk / because / very upset. (might)
....
....
4 Grandpa / be disappointed / if you / not send him / a letter. (will)
....
....
5 Chris / be embarrassed / if Sheena / tell / that story! (might)
....
....
6 Tony / listen / you / because / too jealous. (won't)
....
....
7 Tina / not play / on Saturday / because / has a cold. (might)
....
....

Grammar Reference pages 120–121

Reading

1 Read the text quickly. Match the writers to their opinions.

1 Caitlin a pessimist
2 Brendan b optimist

Send us your comments on the article "Homes of the Future"!

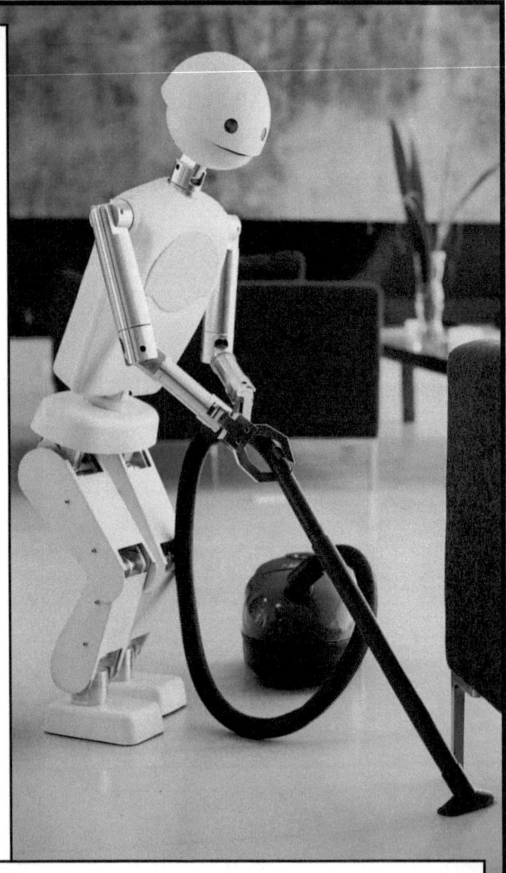

Caitlin says

I feel confident that we'll have robots to do all the chores! I'm fed up with having to do the ironing and take out the trash. I've seen Japanese robots on TV, so I think we might have domestic robots soon. For example, my friend's mom just bought a machine that vacuums the floor by itself. If you don't have to do chores, there's more time to study—and have fun. I also think homes will be much greener, because the buildings will be better, and they'll use clean electricity from the sun, and things like that.

Brendan says

I don't think homes will be so different in the future. Some people might have robots, in the same way that some people now have housecleaners and landscapers to help around the house. But most people will still have to do their own chores. Robots will make you lazy. What will people do with all the extra time? Play more video games? There's nothing wrong with doing a few chores every day: we should all be able to cook and clean, for example. And I'm not sure about greener homes. Maybe some new homes, but not older ones, because people might not have the money to modernize them. In short, I don't think we should expect very big changes.

2 Are the statements true (T) or false (F)?

1 Caitlin doesn't like doing chores. *T*
2 Brendan doesn't mind doing chores. ....
3 Caitlin's friend has to vacuum her home. ....
4 Brendan doesn't think there will be so many robots. ....
5 Caitlin thinks people won't have to study so much. ....

Listening

1 Listen and complete the summary of the conversation. 27

Max is worried because his [1] *sister* is going to college. He says he'll [2]........................ her because there are no other [3]........................ at home. The radio show host says that Max should be more [4]........................ . She says it's a good [5]........................ to talk, but that Max shouldn't forget his [6]........................ from [7]........................ .

2 Match the expression beginnings (1–5) to the endings (a–e). Then listen again and check. 27

1 give you *c*
2 going away ....
3 very lonely ....
4 any other ....
5 a great way ....

a brothers or sisters
b to keep in touch
c some advice
d without her
e to college

Writing • A problem page

1 Rewrite the sentences using *because* or *so*.

1 I can't buy a cell phone because I don't have enough money. (so)
I don't have enough money, so I can't buy a cell phone.

2 They have a dishwasher, so she doesn't have to do the dishes by hand. (because)

....

....

3 You shouldn't get so upset because all friends argue sometimes! (so)

....

....

4 I can't mow the lawn because it's raining! (so)

....

....

5 Everyone went home, so I'm feeling a little lonely. (because)

....

....

6 I can't do so many chores because I have to study! (so)

....

....

2 Read the problem and the advice. Answer the questions.

1 How many reasons with *because* are there?
2 How many results with *so*?

3 Complete column A with details from Ellen's reply.

	A Ellen's reply	B Your reply
Paragraph 1 General advice	Recommendation:	
Paragraph 2 Specific ideas	1 show .... 2 explain .... 3 show .... 4 Mom talk	
Paragraph 3 Ending	Two things to remember: 5 .... 6	

4 Read the following problem. In column B, write your ideas for a reply.

All my friends have smart phones, so they can send each other messages all the time. I don't have one because my parents say I don't need one, and also because they say they're expensive. I would like them to change their mind! What should I do?
Alex

5 Now write your reply to Alex in three paragraphs. Use your ideas and information from Exercises 3 and 4.

Most of my friends at school have an account on a social network, so they're always in touch. They all know what everyone is doing—except me. I'm fed up because I can't talk to my friends or share photos with them! My mom says that it can be dangerous. But nothing has ever happened to my friends! What should I do?

Bethany

Problem Page

Ellen says:

Right, Bethany. Yes, that happens to a lot of teenagers, so we have some ideas to help you. But remember, you mustn't get upset because for many parents social networks are totally new!

The first thing you should do is sit down at the computer with your mom and show her the network because she might not feel very confident about it. And if she doesn't use a computer very often, she won't know how the system works, so you'll have to explain that as well. Maybe you know other members of the family—cousins, for example—who are also on the network. Show your mom their photos, their accounts and how long they've used the network. Then she should talk to your aunt or uncle so she can see she doesn't have to worry about you. Then she'll feel more relaxed.

Finally, don't forget your own responsibilities: keep your passwords secret, and don't accept people you don't know as friends.

Grammar

1 Complete the conversations with the Present perfect or Past simple form of these verbs.

come back	go	have to
hear	~~not see~~	stay

A Hi, Jan! [0] *I haven't seen* you for a while! How are you?
B Fine, thanks!
A You're looking very tanned! [1]........................ (you) to the beach?
B Yes! We [2]........................ (just) from the coast. It was great!
A How long did you stay?
B Ten days. What about you?
A I [3]........................ at home since school ended. My parents [4]........................ work this month, but we're going to Spain next week! Have you been there?
B No, but I [5]........................ about it from friends who have been. It sounds like fun.
A I'll send you a postcard!
B OK!

know	meet	move	not talk	not write

A Who was that?
B That was my friend Ben. I [6]........................ to him for ages! We used to be neighbors.
A How long [7]........................ him?
B Since we lived on the east side of town. Why?
A His face looks familiar. I think I [8]........................ him before.
B When was that?
A At Joanna's birthday party last month.
B Joanna? Tom said I should send her an email, but I [9]........................ it yet.
A You should do it soon, then, because she [10]........................ (just) to another school.
B I didn't know that! Tell me more …

/ 10 points

2 Choose the correct options.

0 Mom says I *don't have to* / *mustn't* have fish for dinner. I can have chicken.
1 The school rules say that we *don't have to* / *mustn't* use cell phones in class.
2 It's not necessary for you to wait any longer. You *don't have to* / *mustn't* wait.
3 You can't wear a T-shirt here. You *have to* / *mustn't* wear a shirt and tie.
4 If you drive in England, remember that you *must* / *don't have to* drive on the left!
5 Uniforms in this school aren't essential. You *don't have to* / *mustn't* wear a uniform.
6 Sorry, cameras aren't allowed in here! You *don't have to* / *mustn't* use a camera here.
7 He *will* / *might* be at home, but I'm not sure.
8 It's 2:30. Tom finishes work at three o'clock, so he *won't* / *might* be at home now.
9 Don't worry, Mom! I promise I *'ll* / *might* call you when I get to the station.
10 I don't know if there's another bus. I *won't* / *might* have to stay the night.

/ 10 points

Vocabulary

3 Choose the correct options.

0 When was the last time you .... camping?
a got **b** did **c** went
1 Did you .... your tan at the beach?
a book **b** get **c** go
2 Have you .... your bags yet?
a packed **b** checked into **c** put up
3 Isn't it your turn to .... the laundry this week?
a clear **b** feed **c** do
4 Oh no! I forgot to .... the dishwasher last night.
a mow **b** load **c** sweep
5 Could you please .... the dog?
a do **b** vacuum **c** walk

/ 5 points

4 **Choose the correct options.**

Did you hear the [0] (report) / *blog* / *newspaper* on the radio this morning? They were talking about this 15-year-old girl who was walking down the street when two men ran out of a store in front of her. Two seconds later, a salesperson appeared, screaming [1] *happily / hard / loudly* for help. The girl was [2] *lonely / confused / guilty* for a moment, but then ran after the men! She followed them down the street and around a corner, and saw them get into a car. She wrote down the license plate number [3] *carefully / carelessly / sadly* and went back to the store. The salesperson called the police, and the men were arrested later that day. The store owner was so [4] *disappointed / fed up / grateful* that he gave the girl a reward. You see? The interesting stories aren't just on the [5] *international news / journalists / news anchors*!

/ 5 points

Speaking

5 **Complete the conversations with these words or phrases.**

~~an argument~~	I don't think you should
kidding	Maybe you should try
strange	Why don't you

A Jared and I had [0] *an argument* last night.
B That's [1] .... You two have always been good friends.
A Yes, I know. But he wants to date me.
B You're [2] .... !
A No, seriously! And I'm not sure about what to do.
B Well, he's a really nice guy. [3] .... going out with him.
A Yes, but it might not work.
B [4] .... worry about that.
A But I don't want to lose a good friend!
B [5] .... think it over this weekend before you make a decision?
A That's a good idea!

get there	How long does it take	Is it far
to buy souvenirs	We're looking for	

A Excuse me! Can you help us?
B Sure! What would you like to know?
A [6] .... the Science Museum. How can we [7] .... ?
B Well, you can walk or take a bus.
A [8] .... ?
B It's about two kilometers.
A [9] .... to get there?
B For young people like you, if you walk, about 15 minutes!
A And is there a good place [10] .... there?
B Yes, the museum has its own gift shop.
A So, which way do we go?

/ 10 points

Translation

6 **Translate the sentences.**

1 I'm sorry, the 6:30 bus just left!
....
2 You're not allowed to put up tents in this area.
....
3 You don't have to come with us if you don't want to.
....
4 Would you mind doing the dishes tonight?
....
5 You won't find any mosquitoes here.
....

/ 5 points

Dictation

7 28 **Listen and write.**

1 ....
2 ....
3 ....
4 ....
5 ....

/ 5 points

7 Make a Difference

Vocabulary • Protest and support

★ **1 Match these words to the definitions (1–6).**

banner	~~charity~~
fundraising event	march
sign	volunteer

1 A non-commercial organization that helps people in difficulty. *charity*
2 A walk by a large group of people, usually to make a protest. ....
3 A large notice with a message on it, usually carried on a stick. ....
4 A person who offers to work without receiving money. ....
5 An activity that people organize in order to collect money. ....
6 A long piece of cloth or paper with a message on it. ....

★ **2 Match the sentence beginnings (1–5) to the endings (a–e).**

1 Would you like to sign *e*
2 We're taking up a collection
3 Would you like to make
4 Can you think of a good
5 Are you coming to the sit-in

a for the homeless people in our town.
b slogan for protecting animals?
c a donation to save tigers?
d at the local theater?
e our petition for safer schools?

★★ **3 Choose the correct options.**

1 Andrea is a *banner* / *volunteer* for a children's charity.
2 That sign has a very clever *donation* / *slogan* on it!
3 Our school is having a *donation* / *fundraising event* this weekend.
4 We have a *collection* / *petition* with 50,000 signatures!
5 The *march* / *sit-in* starts at the station and finishes at town hall.
6 Don't miss the *demonstration* / *donation* in the park at nine o'clock!

★★ **4 Complete the text with these words.**

donation march petition signs ~~sit-in~~ slogans

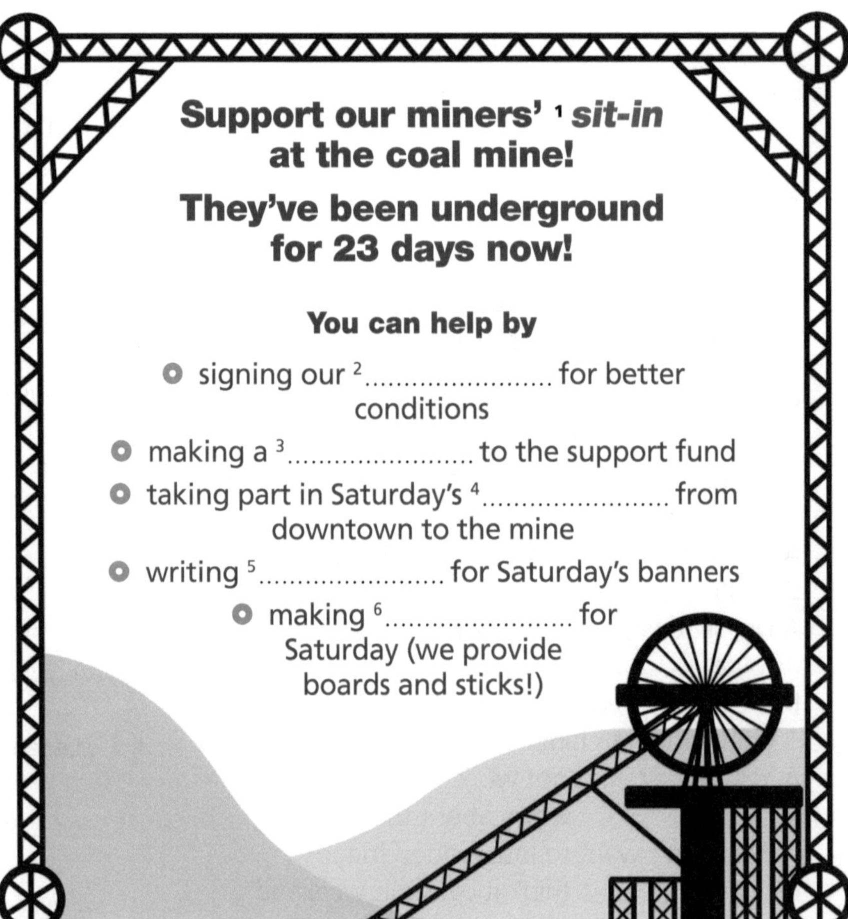

Support our miners' [1] *sit-in* at the coal mine!

They've been underground for 23 days now!

You can help by

- signing our [2]........................ for better conditions
- making a [3]........................ to the support fund
- taking part in Saturday's [4]........................ from downtown to the mine
- writing [5]........................ for Saturday's banners
- making [6]........................ for Saturday (we provide boards and sticks!)

Workbook page 130

★ 1 **Read the text. Match the headings (A–D) to the paragraphs (1–4).**

A What can you do? B What do we do? C Why do we exist? D Who are we?

Integration Now

1 *D*
We're called Integration Now, and we're a local charity that works to help immigrants to adapt to local life. But we would also like local people to meet immigrants, [a] *3* and share their cultures and traditions—without banners, without slogans. We believe that life together is going to be richer and more fun that way.

2 ....
We're here because when you move to another country, it can be very difficult to adapt. You will probably have language problems; you'll often have to [b].... ; your children will go to schools with children from different communities. Even the food [c].... ! So we'd like to help people integrate into their new community.

3 ....
We're a group of volunteers who work from a small office. We give information and advice to immigrants. We take part in local events so that local people can [d].... . Our food festivals are especially popular! And we organize language exchange sessions: you can help people learn your language, and they will teach you some of theirs. Next year [e].... to a bigger space for our own events.

4 ....
You don't have to give donations! Come and [f].... with us. Meet some interesting people. You'll always learn something new!

★ 2 **Match the phrases (1–6) to the blanks (a–f) in the text.**

1 ask for help ....
2 meet immigrants ....
3 get to know them *a*
4 spend some time ....
5 we're going to move ....
6 will be different ....

★★ 3 **Are the statements true (T) or false (F)?**

1 Integration Now works with both immigrants and local people. *T*
2 They organize a lot of marches and protests. ....
3 They mention four common problems for immigrants. ....
4 They work in a local school. ....
5 Not many people go to the food festivals. ....
6 It's not important to help by giving money. ....

Grammar • Be going to

★ **1 Match the questions (1–6) to the answers (a–f).**

1 Is John going to sign the petition? *c*
2 Are you going to join the march?
3 Are your parents going to make signs?
4 What are you going to do with your old laptop?
5 Where's Ted going to study journalism?
6 When are you going to leave school?

a He wants to go to Washington, DC.
b I'll leave at the end of my fourth year.
c He says he is.
d Yes, I am. Definitely!
e I'll probably give it to my cousin.
f Yes. They're going to make six of them.

★ **2 Put the words in the correct order.**

1 **A** birthday / for / going / What / do / are / to / you / your / ?
What are you going to do for your birthday?
B I'll probably have a party.

2 **A** present / What's / to / Tamara / going / ?
....
....
B I think it's a report on sports.

3 **A** teacher / going / exams / When's / the / to / math / grade / the / ?
....
....
B She said she'll grade them next week.

4 **A** collection / Where / take up / are / they / to / the / going / ?
....
....
B They'll probably do it on Main Street.

5 **A** write / are / slogan / for / going / we / to / What / a / ?
....
....
B I'm not really sure. Let's think of something original!

6 **A** invite / Who / you / to / for / are / the / going / weekend / ?
....
....
B A few of my good friends.

★★ **3 Make questions for the underlined answers.**

1 We're going to organize a fundraising event.
What are you going to organize?
2 It's going to be in the community center.
....
3 It's going to start at five o'clock on Saturday.
....
4 Johnny Depp's going to be there.
....
5 We're going to have a poster competition.
....

• *Will* or *be going to*

★ **4 Choose the correct options.**

1 I've read the menu, and *I'll / I'm going to* have the salad.
2 It's Candice's birthday soon. Maybe *we'll / we're going to* get her a present.
3 He's too tired to cook, so *he'll / he's going to* order takeout.
4 Susan said *she'll probably / she's probably going to* go shopping with me.
5 They bought the tickets. After the concert, their parents *will / are going to* pick them up.

★★ **5 Complete the conversation with the correct form of *will* or *going to*.**

A Do you have any plans for next week?
B On Tuesday, my dad and I [1] *are going to* watch the football game on TV. And on Friday, we [2]........................ probably go fishing, but that depends on the weather. What about you?
A The sales start on Monday, so my mom [3]........................ buy me some new clothes. Then on Friday there's a concert.
B Who [4]........................ play at the concert?
A A local band. One of my friends plays the drums.
B Cool! What else are you doing?
A I'm not sure. There's a circus in town this week, so maybe I [5]........................ go to it. And you?
B I can't go out much. I have an exam on Thursday, so I [6]........................ study for that.

Grammar Reference pages 122–123

Vocabulary • Verb + preposition

★ **1 Choose the correct options.**

1 We're going to the demonstration because we don't *agree with* / *argue against* the new law.
2 I really *believe in* / *care about* the environment.
3 We haven't *decided on* / *worried about* a good slogan yet.
4 Ana is *hoping for* / *knows about* a good grade on her exam.
5 We think the factory should *apologize for* / *protest against* causing this pollution!

★ **2 Match the sentence beginnings (1–6) to the endings (a–f).**

1 I can't agree *e*
2 Mike should apologize
3 Anyone who cares
4 It's difficult to decide
5 I don't know anything
6 We're here to protest

a against the plans for another factory in our town.
b about the ice melting in the Arctic.
c for his silly comments.
d about sea life should join the march.
e with your ideas about teenagers.
f on the best place for a day trip.

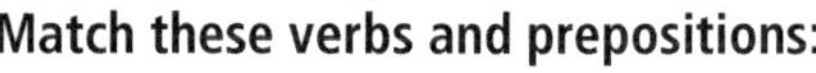

Brain Trainer

Match these verbs and prepositions:

insist	about
believe	on
worry	in

Now do Exercise 3.

★★ **3 Complete the conversation with the correct form of these verbs.**

agree believe disapprove insist ~~protest~~ worry

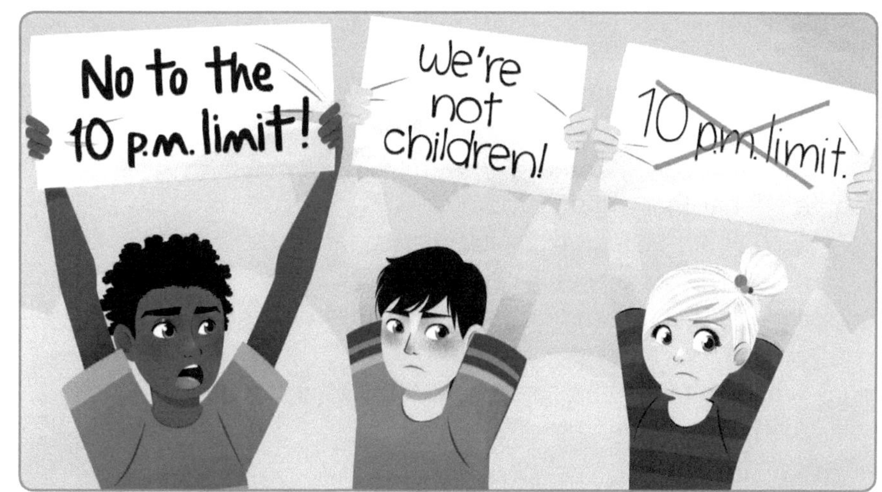

A Hi! What are you [1] *protesting* against?
B We don't [2]........................ with the council's plan to enforce a weekend curfew for teenagers.
A Really? I haven't heard about that.
B They're [3]........................ on 10 p.m. as the latest possible time for teenagers to be out!
A Is that right? I don't think that's really necessary.
B Well, they say they [4]........................ about all the noise for the neighbors. They say they [5]........................ in everyone's right to relax on the weekend, and therefore teenagers should be home before 10 p.m.
A Do you have a petition I can sign?
B Sure! We have a petition for anyone who [6]........................ of the curfew to sign.

★★ **4 Complete the text with the correct prepositions.**

We're planning a march for next Saturday, and we're hoping [1] *for* a crowd of at least 5,000 people to join us. The council wants to build a new landfill in the fields at the edge of town. But we don't believe [2]........................ landfills. We prefer to recycle all the garbage. And we worry [3]........................ the plan, because that area is where many of us have picnics on the weekend. Our representatives have argued [4]........................ them for weeks now, but they insist [5]........................ going ahead with the project. So now is the time to show them how many of us disapprove [6]........................ their idea. They must understand how much we care [7]........................ our environment!

Workbook page 130

Chatroom Persuading

Speaking and Listening

★ 1 **Match the comments (1–6) to the replies (a–f). Then listen and check.**
29

1 Let's go to a demonstration! Come on, it'll be fun. *c*
2 Why don't we join a march? I'm sure you'd enjoy it.
3 Are you coming to the sit-in with us? It's better than sitting at home.
4 How about taking up a collection for cancer research? Come on, it'll be fun.
5 Let's go to a fundraising event! I'm sure you'd enjoy it.
6 Why don't we make some signs? It's better than doing nothing.

a OK, I'll do it! They usually have food and music at those events, don't they?
b OK, I'll do it. Is that the sit-in at the theater?
c I don't know. I've never been to a demonstration before!
d I don't know. I'm not sure we have the right materials.
e OK, let's do it. What's everyone marching for?
f I don't know. The last time I did that, I only collected $10!

★ 2 **Choose the correct options. Then listen and check.**
30

1 Let's go on a march tomorrow! Come (on) / *off*, it'll be fun.
2 How about starting a petition? I'm *think* / *sure* people will sign it!
3 Let's invent slogans! It's better *than* / *that* doing nothing!
4 **A** Why don't we make a banner?
B I don't *think* / *know*. It's very windy outside.
5 **A** How about starting a collection?
B OK, *I'm going to* / *I'll* do it.
6 **A** Do you want to be a volunteer?
B *I'm not sure.* / *I don't think*. It's kind of difficult.

★★ 3 **Complete the conversation with these words. Then listen and check.**
31

I'll do that	it'll be fun	~~I don't know~~
I'm sure	it's better than	

Alex Why don't we go to the demonstration today?
Bea [1] *I don't know*. It's pretty cold out today.
Alex That doesn't matter! We can put warm clothes on.
Bea True, but we don't have a banner.
Alex [2] .... we can make one!
Bea I don't know! I'm kind of tired.
Alex Come on! It's for a good cause, and [3] ....
Bea I guess [4] .... sitting on the sofa! OK, I'll do it. Let's get started on that banner.
Alex [5] .... , and you can make a sign.
Bea OK, sounds great!

★★ 4 **Listen to the conversation in Exercise 3 again. Are the statements true (T) or false (F)?**
31

1 Everything is prepared for the demonstration. *F*
2 Bea isn't sure about the idea. ....
3 Alex says they can buy a banner. ....
4 Alex persuades Bea to go to the demonstration. ....
5 Alex will make the sign. ....

★★ 5 **Write a conversation. Use phrases from Exercises 1–3 and this information:**

You're with a friend. You want to join a protest march, but your friend wants to play a video game instead. Persuade your friend to go to the march with you.

....
....
....
....
....
....
....
....

Speaking and Listening page 135

Grammar • First conditional

★ **1 Match the sentence beginnings (1–6) to the endings (a–f).**

1 If you help me, *e*
2 If you want to stay out late,
3 If you make the banner,
4 We'll clean up the kitchen
5 We'll go on the march
6 We'll plan the party

a if you think of some good slogans.
b if you send the invitations.
c if you cook lunch.
d I'll do the signs.
e I'll help you.
f you'll need to clean up your room first.

★ **2 The Romeo protests. Put the words in the correct order.**

1 What will happen if / us / to / don't / they / listen / ?
What will happen if they don't listen to us?
2 What will happen if / the / stops / the / mayor / demonstration / ?
....
3 If she doesn't come out, / will / march / to / a / organize / we / have
....
4 If she doesn't come out, / slogan / better / a / have / invent / we / to / will
....
5 If she doesn't come out, / need / sign / more / we / to / petition / will / people / the
....

★★ **3 Write sentence endings. Use the correct form of the verbs.**

1 If I do well on these exams, I / get into / the school of my choice.
If I do well on these exams, I'll get into the school of my choice.
2 If you access the webpage, you / get / a lot of good ideas.
....
3 If I don't get home on time, I / miss / my favorite series on TV.
....
4 Her mom will be worried if / she / not come / home on time.
....
5 His father won't be happy if / anything happen / to the car.
....
6 Your pet will get sick if / you / not feed / it properly.
....

★★ **4 Complete the replies with the correct form of the verbs.**

1 **A** What are you worried about?
B If I *don't find* (not find) the house keys, I*'ll be* (be) in trouble!
2 **A** Will you wash the car?
B If I .... (wash) the car, ... (you/give) me some money?
3 **A** Where are my glasses?
B If you .... (look for) them, you .... (find) them!
4 **A** What's the capital of Mongolia?
B .... (you/make) me some coffee if I .... (tell) you the answer?
5 **A** We're meeting at the café at 7:30.
B .... (you/wait for) me if I .... (be) late?
6 **A** Sheena invited you to her party.
B What .... (happen) if I .... (not go)?

Grammar Reference pages 122–123

Reading

1 Read the text quickly and choose the best headline.

a Teenager Gets a Job at a Magazine
b Teenage Protest Produces Results
c Teenagers Support Digital Photos

Who said teenagers don't care about the world around them? Who said that the only thing they worry about is chatting on social networks? Who said that protests never get anywhere? Here's a story to prove those people wrong!

In May 2012, a 13-year-old American girl went to the offices of a well-known teenage magazine to hand in a petition. She went there with her mother and a group of girls who agree with her ideas. What were they protesting against? They said that too many magazine photos show "fake" girls and women. They asked the magazine to be careful about how they use computer programs to change a woman's image. They said that girls need to see "something realistic" when they read their favorite magazines. Julia Bluhm, the 13-year-old, went into the magazine's offices and talked to one of the editors. As a result of that conversation, the magazine has promised to monitor how they process digital photos.

As you can see, protests can achieve results! If you feel strongly about a particular problem, you can talk to your friends and share your opinions. You can start a petition and collect signatures. People will probably listen to you if you present them with reasonable arguments. They might not make *all* the changes you would like, but *something* will happen! So, if you ask yourself "Can we change?," remember what a famous president once said: "Yes we can!"

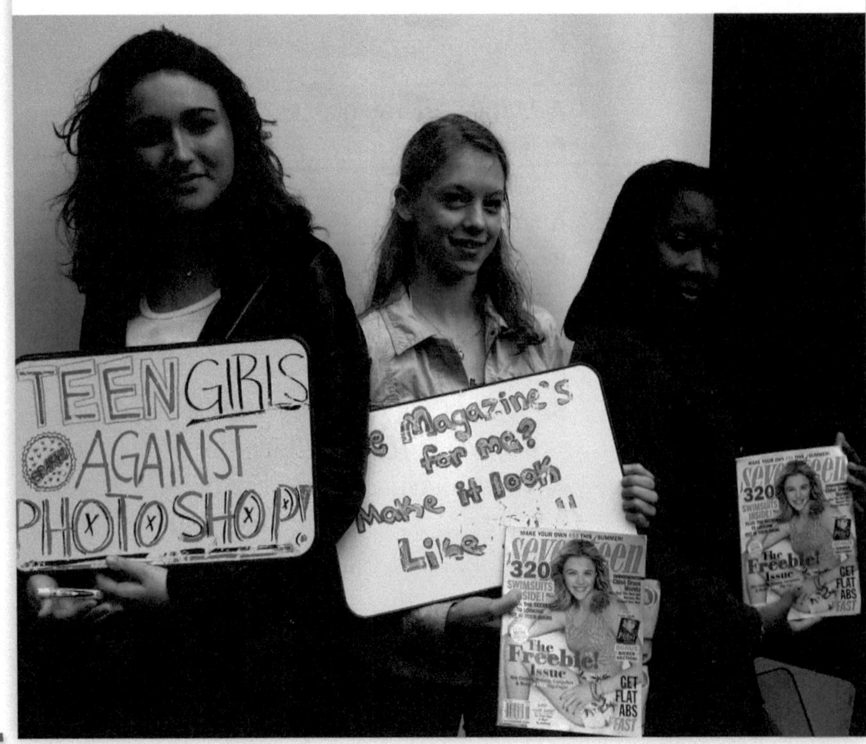

2 Read the text again and choose the correct options.

1 People often say that teenagers *are* / *aren't* interested in current events. (*aren't* circled)
2 Julia Bluhm produced a *petition* / *slogan* for women.
3 Julia and her friends protested against *all* / *some* digital photos.
4 They think that magazine photos of women *are* / *aren't* realistic enough.
5 The article concludes that change *is* / *isn't* possible.

Listening

1 (32) Listen to the conversation. Choose the correct options.

1 The *boy* / *girl* is interested in joining the march. (*girl* circled)
2 The *boy* / *girl* had a friend who went to the hospital.
3 The *boy* / *girl* doesn't worry about the weather.
4 The *boy* / *girl* worries about possible foot pain.
5 The boy decides to go on the march because of the *food* / *good weather*.

2 (32) Who says these phrases? Write B for boy or G for girl. Listen again and check.

1 I can borrow *G*
2 we'll get wet ....
3 these things happen ....
4 I'll probably have to make a new one. ....
5 Didn't I tell you ....
6 All right, you win! ....

Writing • A formal letter

1 Match the letter sections (1–3) to the examples (a–f).

1 Opening
2 Reason for writing
3 Closing

a Kind regards, *3*
b Dear Mr. Jones,
c I am writing to comment on …
d Best wishes,
e Dear *Teenmag,*
f I am writing because …

2 Complete the letter with these phrases.

It is true	like my grandmother	So you see
~~The writer says~~	What can we do	

STAR LETTER

Dear *Teenmag,*

I am writing because I have just read an article in your magazine about older people living alone. [1] *The writer says* that older people should all live together in special homes. I cannot agree with this idea. [2] .... that some older people do not have any family to take care of them, but many of them do. My grandmother lives alone and is very proud of this.

[3] .... to help older people who prefer to live in their own homes? Perhaps we could organize volunteer groups to visit them. If they have company, they will feel better. If we help them, they can teach us a lot too, [4] .... I learn many things from her that I don't learn at school!

[5] .... , it shouldn't be necessary to take older people out of their homes if they prefer to stay there.

Best wishes,
John Noonan

3 Complete column A with information from John's letter.

	A John's letter	B My letter
Reason for writing	*doesn't agree with article*	
The problem		
A possible solution		

4 You recently read an article about pets that have been abandoned in the street. The article said that the animals should be captured and kept in cages at a special shelter. You don't agree with this idea. Write your main ideas in column B.

5 Write a formal letter to express your opinion. Use your ideas and the information and expressions from Exercises 1–4.

....

....
....
....
....
....
....

....
....
....
....
....
....

....
....

8 Danger and Risk

Vocabulary • Extreme adjectives

★ 1 **Complete the sentences with these words.**

~~awful~~	burning	excellent
furious	huge	terrifying

1 The movie wasn't just bad—it was *awful*!
2 The bull we saw wasn't just big—it was .... !
3 The other driver wasn't just angry—he was .... !
4 Walking through the tunnel in total darkness wasn't just scary—it was .... !
5 When we got off the plane in Miami, it wasn't just hot—it was .... !
6 Have you read this? It isn't just good—it's .... !

Brain Trainer

Arrange these adjectives in order of size:
big tiny huge small
Now do Exercise 2.

★ 2 **Replace the <u>underlined</u> words with these adjectives.**

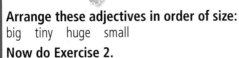

exhausted	~~freezing~~	furious
huge	thrilled	tiny

1 I wasn't wearing enough warm clothes for such a <u>very cold</u> wind. *freezing*
2 We met Beyoncé in a store in New York, and I was <u>really excited</u>. ....
3 At the zoo, I saw a baby kangaroo, and it was <u>very, very small</u>. ....
4 After six hours of shopping, we felt <u>extremely tired</u>. ....
5 A truck crashed into a store and made a <u>really big</u> hole in the wall. ....
6 My parents were <u>really angry</u> when they saw the phone bill. ....

Workbook page 131

★★ 3 **Put the letters in the correct order to complete the text.**

Last winter we did a mountain hike of about 20 kilometers. We walked for hours through the [1] *freezing* (greenfiz) snow, until we reached the top of this mountain. The views from the top were [2]........................ (netlleecx): the people and cars in the distance were just [3]........................ (yint) figures. Then my uncle took us to a special area, where we climbed up into a [4]........................ (eguh) tree. We had to wait half an hour, but then we saw some wild animals come to drink in the small lake. We were [5]........................ (helldirt) because they were so close! And by the time we got back to the car, we were all [6]........................ (steedhaux).

★★ 4 **Complete the conversation with these words.**

awful	burning	excellent
freezing	~~huge~~	tiny

A Did you have a good vacation?
B Yeah, in the end!
A What happened?
B My dad found an apartment building on the Internet that was really cheap. I mean, the building was [1] *huge*: it had 15 floors! But when we got there, we discovered that the apartment itself was [2]........................ for the five of us. It had only two bedrooms and one bathroom!
A Oh no!
B And that's not all! The temperature outside was about 40 degrees Celsius—absolutely [3]........................ . But the air-conditioning inside was really [4]........................ . I was so cold I couldn't sleep!
A Was there anything good about the place?
B Well, the swimming pool was [5]........................ : it wasn't clean enough, and there were too many people. But we were still lucky, because the beach was wonderful, and the nightlife was [6]........................ ! So in the end we didn't really spend much time in the apartment.

Reading

★ 1 **Read the article quickly and answer the question.**

Which person has experienced saving someone? ....

Last week we published an article on risks that people take. This week we asked you the question:

Would you risk your life to save another person or an animal?

Here are some of your replies!

Allie

I don't know! It's difficult to say, because I've never been in such an awful situation. I suppose if a child or a small animal was in trouble, I'd try to help. But I can't imagine that I would risk my life. I mean, I wouldn't jump into a freezing river, because I'm not very strong anyway. And I wouldn't run into a huge burning building either, because that's just too dangerous.

Ben

I'm a little impulsive, so I might do something without thinking too much about it. Last summer at the beach, for example, a little boy fell off a rock, and I was able to rescue him. I was exhausted afterward, but also thrilled. If anything happened to my family or my close friends, I'd probably try to help immediately. But I wouldn't react the same with animals—because I'm not an animal person!

Mannie

I don't think I'd risk my life, but in a terrifying situation, you never know how you'll react. I don't think I'd take any unnecessary risks, but certainly if I thought I could help, I would do so.

★ 2 **Choose the correct options.**

1 Allie (would) / *wouldn't* try to help a child or a small animal.
2 She *would* / *wouldn't* take any serious risks.
3 Ben *often* / *rarely* does things without thinking about them.
4 He *is* / *isn't* into animals.
5 Mannie *is* / *isn't* sure how he would react.

★★ 3 **Are the statements true (T) or false (F)?**

1 Allie has no experience of risking her life. *T*
2 She's pretty sure she's strong enough. ....
3 Ben knows that he would act fast. ....
4 Ben would help both people and animals. ....
5 Mannie would probably try to help if it wasn't too risky. ....

Grammar • Second conditional

★ **1 Match the questions (1–5) to the answers (a–e).**

1 If you had the chance, would you ski down a mountain? *c*
2 If there was an awful fire in the building, would you know what to do?
3 Would you jump into the water if your pet fell into a river?
4 What would you do if you had enough money?
5 Where would you go if you wanted an excellent adventure vacation?

a I don't think I would because I can't swim very well.
b No, I wouldn't. I'd just run for my life.
c I'd love to try, but I don't think I'm brave enough!
d I'd probably go on a safari in Africa.
e I think I'd buy a huge hotel for me, my family and my friends!

★ **2 Match the sentence beginnings (1–5) to the endings (a–e).**

1 If someone gave me a bicycle, *b*
2 If I had to stay in the jungle,
3 If my family had an apartment at the beach,
4 We'd have a bigger dog
5 I'd learn to ride a horse

a I'd go there every weekend!
b I'd use it to go to school.
c I think I'd worry about the snakes.
d if it wasn't so expensive.
e if we had room in our apartment.

★★ **3 Put the words in the correct order to make the questions.**

1 What would happen / if / father's / I / keys / my / car / hid / ?
What would happen if I hid my father's car keys?
2 What would I do / school / if / to / I / go / didn't / today / ?
....
3 If I didn't go to school, / get / would / trouble / I / into / ?
....
4 If I didn't live in my neighborhood, / live / where / would / I / ?
....
5 If I didn't live in my neighborhood, / miss / would / I / it / ?
....
6 What would I buy / if / a lot of / I / had / money / ?
....

★★ **4 Write sentences. Use the Second conditional.**

1 If I weren't so tired, I / stay / watch the movie.
If I weren't so tired, I'd stay to watch the movie.
2 If this book were more interesting, I / finish / reading it.
....
3 If it weren't freezing outside, we / go / for a long walk.
....
4 I'd help you with your homework, if / I / have / more time.
....
5 We'd stay longer, if we / not have to / catch the last bus.
....
6 They'd be much happier, if / it / not rain / so much.
....

★★ **5 Complete the answers with the correct form of the verbs.**

1 **A** Don't you know the answer?
B If I *knew* (know) the answer, I *wouldn't ask* (not ask) you!
2 **A** Do you like the jacket?
B Oh yes! If I .... (have) the money, I .... (buy) it!
3 **A** What's the matter?
B If I .... (have) a map, I .... (not be) lost!
4 **A** Where did you hear that joke?
B You .... (not believe) me if I .... (tell) you!
5 **A** Do you like my new shoes?
B I .... (not wear) them, even if you .... (pay) me to!
6 **A** Should I tell him the truth?
B He .... (be) very disappointed if you .... (lie) to him.

Grammar Reference pages 124–125

Vocabulary • Illness and injury

★ **1 Read the clues and complete the puzzle.**

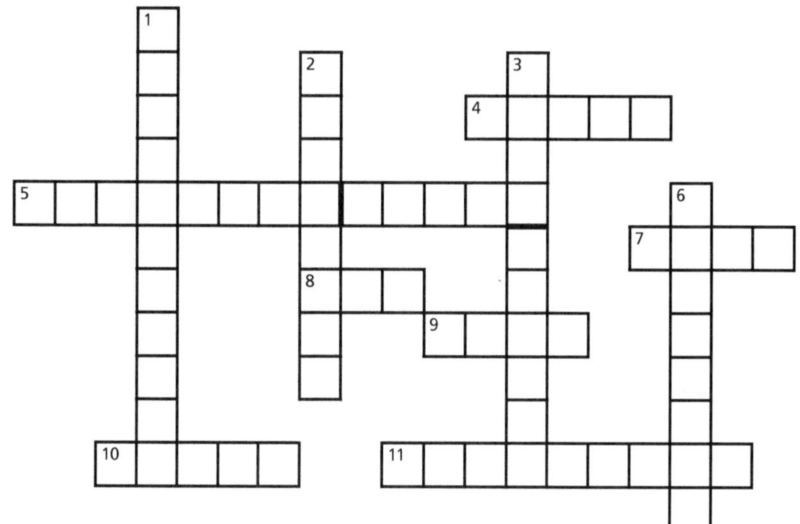

Across

4 This is the noise you make when you force air through your throat.
5 This injury makes it painful to walk.
7 You often get this on your skin if you have an allergy.
8 You might get this on your finger if you have an accident with a knife.
9 You can get this from fire or from the sun!
10 You have this when your body feels too hot.
11 This is a problem for the dentist.

Down

1 This usually happens after you eat too much.
2 When your head hurts.
3 This often happens after shouting too much at a football game.
6 My dad got this when he was moving heavy furniture.

★ **2 Complete the doctor's sentences with these words.**

a cough   a backache   a fever
a rash   ~~a sprained ankle~~

1 I was walking down the street when I put my foot in a hole and fell down.
You have *a sprained ankle*.
2 My dad was lifting a big suitcase, and now he has this pain.
He has ....
3 I woke up during the night and couldn't stop making this noise.
You had ....
4 My legs are covered with little red marks!
You have ....
5 I'm too hot, I don't feel well, and I'm really thirsty.
You have ....

★★ **3 Match the problems (1–5) to the suggestions (a–e).**

1 a burn *e*
2 a cut
3 a sore throat
4 a stomachache
5 a toothache

a Why don't you take some of this medicine?
b You should go to the dentist!
c Don't eat or drink anything until you feel better.
d You should cover that with a bandage.
e Put a lot of cold water on it.

★★ **4 Put the letters in the correct order to complete the teacher's report.**

Most of the students this winter have had the usual 1 *coughs* (hugsoc) and 2 .... (dolcs). Three of them have come to class with a 3 .... (refve), so I had to send them home. Many of them also complained about 4 .... (shadecahe), probably because of the heating in the school. One boy showed up with a 5 .... (nurb) on his hand, obviously from playing with matches. But nobody has had any 6 .... (shears) this year.

What's the matter?

Workbook page 131

Chatroom Talking about health

Speaking and Listening

★ **1** (33) **Choose the correct options. Then listen and check.**

1 What's the *ache* / *matter*?
2 I have a sprained *nose* / *ankle*.
3 *Are* / *Do* you all right?
4 How *do* / *does* it feel?
5 Not too *good* / *better*.
6 How *do* / *does* you feel?
7 A little *better* / *worse*, thanks.

★ **2** (34) **Put the sentences in the correct order. Then listen and check.**

a What's the matter, Monica? ..1..
b It means you won't be able to walk for at least a week. ....
c You have a sprained ankle. ....
d Does this hurt? ....
e Oww! Yes, it does. ....
f What does that mean? ....
g Oh no! ....
h I was hiking in the woods when I tripped on a rock. ....

★★ **3** (35) **Complete the conversation with these phrases. Then listen and check.**

a little better now	do you feel	does it feel
~~I burned myself~~	That's awful	the matter

Jess That looks painful! What happened to you?
Jack [1] *I burned myself* in the kitchen.
Jess What were you doing?
Jack I was helping to cook lunch. Fried fish.
Jess So?
Jack The fish slipped out of my fingers, and I got burning hot oil all over my hand.
Jess [2]........................ ! What did you do?
Jack My mom turned the faucet on, and I held my hand under the running water. Then we got a cloth with some ice in it, and came straight here to see the doctor.
Jess How [3]........................ ?
Jack It's still a little painful. But what about you? What's [4]........................ with your hand?
Jess I was cutting up vegetables, and the knife slipped.
Jack How [5]........................ ?
Jess Well, I was kind of scared because I don't like seeing blood. But I'm feeling [6]........................ , thanks.
Jack That's good. I hate seeing blood, too!

★★ **4** (35) **Listen to the conversation in Exercise 3 again. Mark (✓) the correct box.**

	Jack	Jess	Both
1 accident in the kitchen			✓
2 hot oil			
3 kitchen knife			
4 used cold water			
5 went to the doctor			

★★ **5** **Write a conversation. Use phrases from Exercises 1–3 and this information:**

You go to visit a friend, and you find him/her sick in bed. Talk about his/her health. Explain something similar which happened to you last year.

Speaking and Listening page 136

Grammar • Relative pronouns

★ **1 Match the sentence beginnings (1–6) to the endings (a–f).**

1 That's the stadium *e*
2 That's the singer
3 There's the store
4 This is the pump
5 She's the journalist
6 That's the wall

a who wrote the article.
b which I use for my bike.
c which I fell off.
d where I bought my bike.
e where our team won the championship.
f who gave me an autograph.

★ **2 Choose the correct options.**

1 These are the photos *where* / *which* (circled) we took on vacation.
2 This is the guide *which* / *who* showed us around the city.
3 This is the restaurant *where* / *which* we had my birthday dinner.
4 These are the Chinese students *which* / *who* visited our school today.
5 This is the entrance to the theme park *where* / *which* I told you about.
6 Here's the river *where* / *which* we took a boat trip.

★ **3 Complete the conversation with *who, which* or *where.***

A Who are the people in this picture?
B They're the ones [1] *who* went on the skiing trip.
A What happened to that boy on the left?
B He's the one [2] .... got a sprained ankle on the first day!
A What a shame! And what's that in the girl's hand?
B That's the helmet [3] .... she wore to protect her head.
A And in the background?
B That's the park [4] .... we had a picnic lunch.
A What's that black thing there?
B That's the place [5] .... we made a small fire to keep warm!
A Nice! And are those your skis?
B No, they're the ones [6] .... I borrowed from another student. They were much better than mine!

★★ **4 Make sentences with *who, which* or *where.***

1 This is the dog / bite me / when / we be / on vacation.
This is the dog which bit me when we were on vacation.
2 This is the park / everything happen.
....
3 Here's the car / my father / take me / to the hospital / in.
....
4 This is the doctor / look at / my leg.
....
5 That's the needle / he use / to give me a shot.
....
6 This is the nurse / put a bandage / on the bite.
....

Grammar Reference pages 124–125

Reading

1 **Read the questions and choose the best answer.**

2 **Read the score box and check your answers.**

Listening

1 **Listen and answer the questions.** 36

1 There are .... people in the conversation.
   a 2 (b) 3 c 4

2 They're talking .... .
   a in the hospital
   b at home
   c at the doctor's office

3 The boy had a .... accident.
   a walking
   b bicycle
   c car

4 He has problems with his .... .
   a knee and legs
   b eyes and neck
   c stomach and back

5 The doctor checked the injuries .... .
   a immediately
   b after an hour
   c after two hours

2 **Who says these phrases? Write M for mother, S for son or U for uncle. Listen again and check.** 36

1 I'm much better S
2 an awful accident ....
3 sprained his knee ....
4 How did it feel? ....
5 Not too good! ....
6 How did it happen? ....

Would you know how to survive in an extreme environment?

Answer our questionnaire and find out!

1 If you got lost in the jungle, what would you do?
a make a fire with a lot of smoke
b find a river and follow it downstream
c climb a big tree to check your location

2 If you were exhausted after walking in deep snow and it got dark, what would you do?
a dig a hole in the snow and sleep inside it
b lie down behind a big rock and sleep
c try to stay awake and keep walking

3 If you were on a mountain and a terrifying storm began, what would you do?
a get off the mountain as quickly as possible
b keep walking until you found a cave
c sit under a big tree until the storm passed

4 If you were walking in a meadow and met a huge bull, what would you do?
a walk backward slowly and carefully
b stand completely still and wait for the bull to go away
c turn around and run away

5 If you sprained your ankle in the mountains, what would you do?
a try to find an area with a signal for your cell phone
b use a mirror to make SOS signals in the sun
c make a fire with a lot of smoke

Score

a = 3 points **b** = 2 points **c** = 1 point

11–15 points: Congratulations! You know the right things to do!
6–10 points: You need to review your options.
1–5 points: You have a lot to learn!

Writing • An application form

1 **Match the question words (1–6) to the answers (a–f).**

1 Who *f*
2 What
3 Where
4 When
5 Why
6 How many

a because that's our timetable!
b twenty-five
c school assembly
d in the auditorium
e at 8:30 in the morning
f my class

2 **Make questions for the underlined words.**

1 There are five people in my family.
How many people are there in your family?
2 We live in an apartment near a park.
....
3 No, I've never been abroad.
....
4 I'd like to go because I think it would be interesting.
....
5 I play soccer with my friends.
....
6 I'll be 15 next April.
....

3 **Read the application form. Are the statements true (T) or false (F)?**

1 Max can't run very fast. *T*
2 He's had several pets. ....
3 He probably likes taking risks. ....
4 He's not into rhinos. ....
5 He probably wouldn't know what to do in an emergency in the park. ....

4 **Now complete the application form yourself.**

LITTLE AFRICA SAFARI PARK

Application form

Name: *Max Williams* Age: *15*

1 How many of these things can you do? Mark the boxes.
swim ☑ run fast ☐ climb trees ☑
use a canoe ☐ take underwater photos ☐

2 How many of these things have you done? Mark the boxes. Say when you did them.
take care of a pet ☐ ....
visit the zoo ☑ *I went last year on a school field trip.*
work with animals ☐ ....
go abroad ☑ *I went to France in 2014.*

3 What kind of person do people say you are? Circle three words.
(quiet) noisy shy (adventurous) thoughtful impulsive patient (impatient)

4 Which animals would you prefer NOT to see? Mark the boxes. Say why.
camels ☐ crocodiles ☐ hyenas ☑ lions ☐ rhinos ☐ snakes ☑
Hyenas are really ugly, and I'm afraid of snakes.

5 Write three things you would like to do in the safari park.
1 *ride a camel*
2 *see a crocodile*
3 *take photos*

6 Have you read the safety instructions in the visitors' guide? Yes ☐ No ☑

LITTLE AFRICA SAFARI PARK

Application form

Name: .... Age: ....

1 How many of these things can you do? Mark the boxes.
swim ☐ run fast ☐ climb trees ☐
use a canoe ☐ take underwater photos ☐

2 How many of these things have you done? Mark the boxes. Say when you did them.
take care of a pet ☐ ....
visit the zoo ☐ ....
work with animals ☐ ....
go abroad ☐ ....

3 What kind of person do people say you are? Circle three words.
quiet noisy shy adventurous thoughtful impulsive patient impatient

4 Which animals would you prefer NOT to see? Mark the boxes. Say why.
camels ☐ crocodiles ☐ hyenas ☐ lions ☐ rhinos ☐ snakes ☐
....

5 Write three things you would like to do in the safari park.
1 ....
2 ....
3 ....

6 Have you read the safety instructions in the visitors' guide? Yes ☐ No ☐

Inventions

Vocabulary • Machine nouns and verbs

★ **1 Match the sentence beginnings (1–6) to the endings (a–f).**

1 This product will run on a battery, *e*
2 To turn on the machine,
3 Then use the keyboard
4 To attach files to an email,
5 If you want to watch TV,
6 Don't forget to turn off

a press the round button in the corner.
b click on the "Attach" button at the bottom.
c the machine when you've finished.
d you can also use the remote control.
e or you can plug the power cord into an outlet.
f to type in your password.

★★ **2 Put the letters in the correct order to complete the sentences.**

1 Has anyone seen the *remote control* (meteor clorton)? I need it to change channels!
2 You can't play a car racing game without a .... (hewel) to move the car!
3 Oh no! The .... (trytabe) has died in the middle of the game!
4 It probably goes faster if you use the .... (beardyok) controls.
5 You have to plug in the power .... (rodc) first to turn the TV on.
6 If you press that .... (tontub), you'll delete all your work!
7 Take the cord out of the .... (teluto) before you go to bed!
8 This is a special plastic .... (beut) to keep all the electric cords in.

Workbook page 132

★ **3 Complete the conversation with these words.**

button	cable	jack	plugged it in
press	~~remote control~~		turned it on

A What are you doing?
B We're trying to watch a movie, but we can't open the file.
A Have you selected the file with the [1] *remote control*?
B Yes, that's it there.
A Have you checked the [2] .... ?
B Which one?
A The one that goes from the computer to the TV.
B Yes, John [3] ....
A Yes, but is it in the right [4] .... ?
B I don't know!
A OK, I changed it. Now [5] .... the "Enter" [6] ....
B Hey! It's open! But I can't hear anything!
A You need to check the volume control then. Have you [7] .... ?
B Yes, that's it now. Thanks!

★★ **4 Complete the text with the correct form of these verbs.**

attach	~~communicate~~	invent
plug in	press	turn off

How do you [1] *communicate* with your friends? Sending emails was OK, until someone [2] .... text messages on cell phones. Now cell phones do the same things as a computer, and they're much more convenient (unless you forget to [3] .... the battery to recharge!). Touch screens are amazing: you don't even have to [4] .... buttons anymore! I also use a special application that works with Wi-Fi. I can chat with my friends, and it's very cheap. But it can be expensive if you forget to [5] .... the Internet access or if you [6] .... a lot of photos or videos to a message.

Reading

★ 1 **Read the text and put the paragraphs in the correct order.**

1 C 2 .... 3 .... 4 .... 5 ....

A In the second stage, the drawings are computerized by the keyboard programmers. This is when the characters start to move. Then all the colors are attached, so the places and movements look real. These are like the building blocks for the whole game.

B The final stage is just as important as the other ones: game testing. A selection of players are asked to use the game and communicate any operating problems they find. Once these problems are solved, the game is ready for you to turn on and play!

C Most of us have shared an afternoon playing video games with friends, but how many of us know how the games are made? Let me tell you about the process in four basic stages.

D In the third stage, the parts of the story are put in order. Next, the player options are produced. This is done by specialized programmers. So now the game has its two key parts: the different levels of difficulty and all the tasks for the players.

E First of all, you should know that most games are produced by a team who work closely together. They have a lot of meetings where the basic story and characters are discussed. Once these components are agreed on, artists produce a set of drawings. The drawings illustrate the characters and the places in the game—for example, an old castle, a sports stadium or a futuristic city.

★ 2 **Who does what? Match the actions (1–5) to the people (a–e).**

1 invent the story and characters *d*
2 make the first drawings
3 computerize the drawings
4 create the options for players
5 check the game for problems

a a group of players
b keyboard programmers
c specialized programmers
d the team
e artists

★★ 3 **Are the statements true (T) or false (F)?**

1 One person is responsible for the story. *F*
2 The characters' movements are built in the second stage. ....
3 Programmers do their jobs in the second and third stages. ....
4 Most video games have three main parts. ....
5 The testing stage is the most important one. ....
6 Most games are developed in four different stages. ....

Grammar • Present simple passive

★ **1 Choose the correct options.**

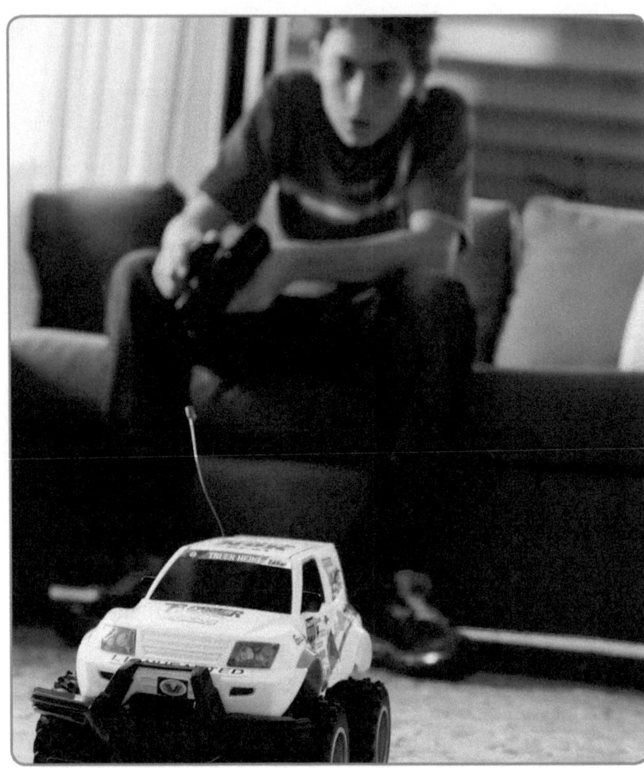

Radio-controlled cars [1] *is* / *are* operated by a remote control. Two sets of batteries [2] *is* / *are* needed for the toy to function correctly. A large battery [3] *is* / *are* located in the body of the car, and a smaller battery [4] *is* / *are* placed in the remote control. A radio signal [5] *is* / *are* sent from the remote control to the car. The speed and direction of the car [6] *is* / *are* controlled by the buttons you press on the remote control.

★★ **2 Match the sentence beginnings (1–6) to the endings (a–f).**

1 First, the cars are *e*
2 Next, the design is
3 Then the parts are
4 Next, they are
5 Then everything is
6 Finally, the new cars are

a checked by computer.
b transported to the showrooms.
c produced in a factory.
d assembled in another factory.
e designed in the laboratory.
f created by the engineers.

★★ **3 Complete the questions, then add the correct answers.**

1 *Are* cars made in Korea?
Yes, *they are.*
2 .... olive oil produced in England?
No, ...
3 .... cell phones repaired here?
No, ...
4 .... phone batteries sold separately?
Yes, sometimes ....
5 .... rice grown in China?
Yes, ...
6 .... batteries provided with all your products?
No, ...
7 .... these TVs equipped with the necessary cables?
Yes, some of them ....

★★ **4 Make questions.**

1 **A** Where / the best cars / produce?
Where are the best cars produced?
B In Germany!
2 **A** these oranges / grow / locally?
....
B No, they aren't.
3 **A** How / this program / install / on the computer?
....
B By following the instructions on the screen!
4 **A** Why / the cables / not provide / with the TVs?
....
B Because different people use different cables!
5 **A** Where / those watches / sell?
....
B Only in specialized shops.
6 **A** How / these trucks / build?
....
B I really don't know!

• Active and passive

★ **5 Rewrite the sentences in the passive. Include *by* + noun only if necessary.**

1 People in Italy design these clothes.
These clothes are designed in Italy.

2 Our chef prepares all our famous dishes.
....
....
....
....

3 Someone sells CDs like those in the street market.
....
....
....
....

4 We ask passengers not to stand near the doors.
....
....
....
....

5 The president of the club writes these articles.
....
....
....
....

6 People usually cook this kind of meat in a spicy sauce.
....
....
....
....

7 Shakira sings all the songs on this album.
....
....
....
....

Grammar Reference pages 126–127

Vocabulary • Word building

★ **1 Choose the correct options.**

1 Cell phones have been a very popular *inventor* / *invention*.
2 Who was the *designer* / *design* of the first MP3 players?
3 We visited the capital, and we loved the old *builders* / *buildings* there.
4 Cars and video games are some of Japan's most famous *producers* / *products*.
5 Monet is one of my favorite *painters* / *paintings*.
6 I'd love to know more about where *writers* / *writing* came from.

★ **2 Look at the text on page 109. Find nouns for the verbs (1–5).**

1 move *movements*
2 select ....
3 play ....
4 program ....
5 draw ....

★★ **3 Complete the words with the correct ending.**

1 I think the computer is the most important invent*ion* of all time.
2 For me, Goya is the most original paint....... of all time.
3 My mom doesn't like these modern build....... ; she prefers old ones.
4 Our company sells only top-quality prod....... .
5 Armani is my sister's favorite fashion design....... .
6 What does this note say? I can't read the writ....... .

★★ **4 Complete the conversations with the correct form of these words.**

build (x2)	~~design~~	invent	produce (x2)	write (x2)

1 **A** Why are these shoes so expensive?
B Because they're *designed* by Christian Louboutin!
2 **A** Who were the .... of the great cathedrals?
B Nobody really knows their names!
3 **A** Why are these called personalized poems?
B Because they're specially .... for individual people.
4 **A** What does a movie .... do?
B He or she finds the money to make the movie.
5 **A** Who was the .... of TV?
B A man named John Logie Baird.
6 **A** Are these houses strong?
B I hope so! They're .... of concrete and brick.
7 **A** What kind of .... is this? I've never seen it before.
B It looks like Chinese.
8 **A** What kind of .... are made here?
B We make boots and shoes.

Workbook page 132

Speaking and Listening

★ **1** 37 **Match the questions (1–5) to the answers (a–e). Then listen and check.**

1 What's the problem? *b*
2 Have you checked the battery?
3 Have you checked the earphones?
4 There might be something wrong with the connection.
5 Have you checked that it's plugged in?

a No, I haven't, and it's not. Yikes! I forgot!
b My MP3 player doesn't work.
c It's OK. I've checked it.
d They worked all right this morning.
e Yes, I bought a new one yesterday.

★ **2** 38 **Choose the correct options. Then listen and check.**

A You don't look very happy! What's the problem?
B The projector doesn't [1] *move* / *work*.
A Are you sure? I used it on the weekend.
B Well, it's turned [2] *on* / *off*, but it's not showing the movie.
A There might be something [3] *problem* / *wrong* with the cable.
B I don't think so. It's plugged properly into the [4] *battery* / *jack*.
A Have you [5] *broken* / *checked* the F5 button?
B Oh, right! That's it! You're a genius!

★ **3** 39 **Complete the conversation with these phrases. Then listen and check.**

~~broken~~	checked them
I haven't tried that	pressed the button
see the images	something wrong

A What's the problem?
B My digital camera is [1] *broken*.
A Are you sure? You were taking photos yesterday.
B I know, but not anymore.
A There might be [2] .... with the battery.
B I've checked that, and it's OK.
A Have you [3] .... to turn it on?
B Yes! Look, the blue light's on.
A What about the settings? Have you [4] .... ?
B What settings?
A The symbols on the wheel.
B Ah no! [5] ....
A Well, try turning it around, to check the different symbols.
B Wait a minute. Now I can see the image on the screen!
A Let me look. Ah, you had the wrong setting. That's why you couldn't [6] ....

★★ **4** 39 **Listen to the conversation in Exercise 3 again. Write the three things they checked.**

1 ....
2 ....
3 ....

★★ **5** **Write a conversation. Use phrases from Exercises 1–3 and this information:**

A friend is having a problem with his/her video game console. Ask your friend to explain the problem; make suggestions about how to solve the problem.

....
....
....
....

Speaking and Listening page 137

Grammar • Past simple passive

★ **1 Complete the questions and answers.**

1 *Was* the first smart phone produced in 1994?
Yes, *it was*.
2 .... more laptops than desktops sold in 2008?
Yes, ...
3 .... digital cameras invented in Japan?
No, ...
4 .... the first TV built in the US?
No, ...
5 .... your CDs replaced by MP3s?
Yes, ...

★★ **2 Complete the sentences with the correct form of these verbs.**

catch	fly	forget	grow
keep	sell	sing	~~write~~

1 This famous book was *written* by Tolkien.
2 These songs were .... only on special occasions.
3 Some scrolls were .... in libraries for hundreds of years.
4 Kites were .... for the first time in ancient China.
5 Thanks to the invention of books, old stories were not ....
6 Fish were .... here until the river became too polluted.
7 The palace was .... because the family needed the money.
8 Cotton was .... in ancient Egypt.

Brain Trainer

Notice what happens to the position of the main noun when a sentence is transformed from active to passive.

Active: Tolkien wrote *this book*.
Passive: *This book* was written by Tolkien.

★★ **3 Make questions.**

1 **A** cars / invent / in Germany?
Were cars invented in Germany?
B Probably, but I'm not sure.
2 **A** When / Lady Gaga's first album / release?
....
B That was in 2008!
3 **A** When / Michael Jackson's last concert / hold?
....
B I think that was in 1997.
4 **A** Which famous English musician / kill / New York in 1980?
....
B It was John Lennon.
5 **A** What / Stephenie Meyer's first book / call?
....
B *Twilight*. It's her best-known book.

★★ **4 Rewrite the sentences in the passive. Include *by* + noun only if necessary.**

1 Americans reelected Barack Obama president in 2012.
Barack Obama was reelected president in 2012.
2 A tornado destroyed ten houses last week.
....
....
3 Police rescued three children from the ocean on Monday.
....
....
4 Someone stole the school sports trophies last night!
....
....
5 A teacher saw three cats on the school roof this morning.
....
....
6 Ten thousand people signed the petition to keep the local library open.
....
....

Grammar Reference pages 126–127

Reading

1 Read the texts quickly and match the names (1–3) to their preferences (a–c).

1 Natalia	a cars
2 Ted	b electric guitars
3 Chris	c Internet

Last week we asked you to tell us about your favorite inventions. Here is a selection of your replies.

Natalia

For me, the greatest invention ever is the car! Life wouldn't be the same without cars. Obviously, I don't drive yet, but I help my dad with our car. We watch Formula 1 races on TV, and sometimes we go to see the real thing if there's a race in our area. I get car magazines and read about the latest models. When I'm older, I'd really like to buy a red German sports car.

Ted

My favorite invention is the Internet! Laptops and smart phones are fun, but it's the Internet that makes everything possible. I can use it for entertainment, but also to study with. My parents do a lot of shopping on the Internet, too. But above all, I use it for social networking: I have to know where my friends are and what they're doing!

Chris

I'd say that electric guitars are my favorite invention. If we didn't have them, we wouldn't have any concerts, and life would be boring! Concerts are really important for me; they have such an atmosphere, and unlike CDs, you can really feel the music. But I also play the guitar and spend a lot of time practicing with friends. I learn a lot from watching the guitarists on TV, too.

2 Are the statements true (T) or false (F)?

1 Natalia only sees car races on TV. *F*
2 Ted uses the Internet for three different reasons. ....
3 Chris thinks studio music is the best. ....
4 Natalia also plays a musical instrument. ....
5 Ted's main priority is contact with his friends. ....
6 Chris's main priority is music. ....

Listening

1 40 **Listen and complete the summary of the conversation. Use one word in each space.**

Ally helps Ben, who has a problem with the [1] *video*. First they check the [2]........................ cord, then the [3]........................ cable and finally the [4]........................ cable. Next, Ally suspects there might be something wrong with the input source on the [5]........................ . In the end, she uses the [6]........................ to solve the problem.

2 40 **Listen again and put these phrases in the order you hear them.**

a in the wrong place ....
b the hard drive ....
c the power cord ....
d Here you go. ....
e It's both, actually. *1*

Writing • An opinion essay

1 Put the parts of an opinion essay in the correct order.

a Second, using an e-book, you don't have to carry so many heavy schoolbooks. ....
b In my opinion, e-books are a really important invention. ....
c In conclusion, our life would be much simpler if we used more e-books. ....
d First, many different books can be stored in them. ....
e An important invention *1*
f Finally, e-books save huge amounts of paper and trees. ....

2 Complete the opinion essay with these phrases.

fast and safe	~~important inventions~~
my social life	that's not true
the other traffic	

An invention I couldn't live without

In my opinion, there are many [1] important inventions, but I couldn't live without my mountain bike.

First, it's my normal means of transportation. I use it to go to and from school every day. It's [2] .... , it doesn't cost anything, and unlike [3] .... , it doesn't pollute the air. In fact, I have to be careful not to breathe all the fumes from the traffic!

Second, it's a great way to get exercise. Everyone talks about teenagers sitting on sofas playing video games and eating the wrong kind of food, but [4] .... for all of us!

Finally, it's an important part of [5] .... For example, on weekends I go out on trips with friends, and if I didn't have my bike, I wouldn't know so many people!

In conclusion, my life wouldn't be the same without my bike.

3 You are going to write an essay with the same title. Complete the table with your ideas.

An invention I couldn't live without	
Paragraph 1: introduction	1 ....
Paragraphs 2–4: reasons and example(s)	2 .... 3 .... 4 ....
Paragraph 5: conclusion	5 ....

4 Now write an opinion essay. Use your ideas, and information and expressions in Exercises 1–3.

....
....
....
....
....
....
....
....
....
....
....
....
....
....
....

Check 3

Grammar

1 Choose the correct options.

0 Tell me your plan! What .... do now?
a will you **b** are you **c** are you going to (circled)

1 Her mom says that Sue .... leave until she's finished cleaning up her room.
a won't **b** doesn't **c** isn't going to

2 I don't think I .... pizza—I'm tired of pizza!
a 'll have **b** won't have **c** 'm going to have

3 They've already decided: they .... write to the newspaper.
a 'll **b** are going **c** are

4 Here's the woman .... gave us the tickets for the concert!
a where **b** which **c** who

5 These are the presents .... we bought for Dad.
a where **b** which **c** who

/ 5 points

2 Make sentences.

0 She / take you shopping if you ask her nicely!
She will take you shopping if you ask her nicely!

1 If you don't help me with the housework, I / not / give you a ride in the car.
....
....

2 If I / know / how to repair the camera, I'd do it for you!
....
....

3 If you don't leave some money for the waiter, he / not be / very happy!
....
....

4 What would happen if / not rain / all year?
....
....

5 If you had to go to school on Saturdays, what / you do / on Sundays?
....
....

/ 5 points

3 Complete the text with the passive forms of the verbs.

The world's first airplane took off in 1903 and began the race for better air machines. Many new kinds of planes [0] *were developed* (develop) between the two world wars. Jets and helicopters [1] .... (build) during World War II, and the first commercial jet flight [2] .... (achieve) in the 1950s. The Concorde, the world's fastest commercial plane, [3] .... (run) between 1969 and 2003. However, this kind of jet [4] .... (not produce) anymore. Today modern airplanes [5] .... (design) to use less fuel.

/ 5 points

Vocabulary

4 Complete the sentences with these words.

agree with	argue with	believe in
~~care about~~	signs	slogans

0 I signed the petition because I *care about* my community.

1 We spent all morning making the .... for the demonstration.

2 We wrote .... for our banners.

3 People join a march because they .... the reasons it was organized.

4 If we don't .... other people, there will never be any change.

5 I'm sorry, I don't .... your ideas!

/ 5 points

5 Choose the correct options.

0 **A** Why can't he walk very well?
B He has a *stomachache / toothache / sprained ankle.* (circled: sprained ankle)

1 **A** Did you enjoy the movie?
B Yes. It was *awful / excellent / burning hot*!

2 **A** What's wrong with your hand?
B I have a *cough / cold / rash.*

3 **A** Isn't that pizza awfully big?
B Big? It's positively *huge / freezing / thrilled*.

4 **A** I couldn't hear very well at the theater.
B Why not?
A The woman behind me had a *headache / burn / cough*.

5 **A** Have you read this story?
B No, and I'm not going to. I've heard it's *furious / terrifying / exhausted*.

/ 5 points

6 Choose the correct options.

0 It won't work unless you turn this little .... here.
a tube **(b)** wheel **c** keyboard

1 No wonder it doesn't work! It's not .... !
a plugged in **b** produced **c** invented

2 Nowadays many people .... through chats and blogs.
a attach **b** build **c** communicate

3 If you have problems with a power cord, try checking the .... .
a batteries **b** outlet **c** buttons

4 What was the name of the artist who produced this .... ?
a paint **b** painter **c** painting

5 Historians have discovered the name of the original .... of the monument.
a design **b** designer **c** designation

/ 5 points

Speaking

7 Complete the conversation with one word in each blank.

A What's the problem?
B My cell phone doesn't [0] *work*. I can't make a call.
A Have you [1]........................ the battery?
B Yes, of course! Look!
A Have you tried [2]........................ the message button?
B No, I haven't.
A Well, this message [3]........................ you don't have coverage! Anyway, what's the [4]........................ with Ethan?
B He hasn't stopped working all week.
A [5]........................ does he feel?
B He says he feels exhausted—and he has a [6]........................ throat.
A Maybe he [7]........................ lie down for a while. So, will we go out for dinner?
B I don't know. What about Ethan?
A He'll be fine! [8]........................ on, it's only an hour or two.
B I shouldn't leave him alone.
A Why not? It's [9]........................ than staying at home.
B I'll tell you what. We'll get takeout, and then we can eat here together.
A OK, you win! [10]........................ do that.

/ 10 points

Translation

8 Translate the sentences.

1 If we don't protest, no one will change anything!
....

2 What kind of slogan are you going to write?
....

3 The first car was invented by Karl Benz.
....

4 What would you do if you had a stomachache?
....

5 If I were you, I'd check the battery in the laptop.
....

/ 5 points

Dictation

9 Listen and write.
41

1 ....
2 ....
3 ....
4 ....
5 ....

/ 5 points

Grammar Reference

• Present perfect + *for* and *since*; *How long?*

How long have we been here? We've been here for five days/a week/a month.
I haven't read a book since Saturday.
She's lived in France since 2010.

Use

We use the Present perfect with *for* to indicate a period of time:
We've been on vacation for two weeks.

We use the Present perfect with *since* to indicate a point in time:
We've been on vacation since Monday the 14th.

We use *How long?* to ask about the duration of an action:
***How long have you been** on vacation?*
***How long have you lived** here?*

• Past simple with *just*

You just had ice cream.
You just missed the train.
The menu just changed.

Use

We use the Past simple with *just* to indicate an action that happened a short time ago:
*The six o'clock train **just left**. (It's 6:03 now.)*
*I **just went** to the bank. (Here's the money I got.)*

Grammar practice • Present perfect + *for* and *since*; *How long?*

1 Choose the correct options.

1 We've lived here (*for*) / *since* six years.
2 I haven't heard that song *for* / *since* we were in Hawaii!
3 I haven't visited Germany *for* / *since* I was a child.
4 Our families have gone camping together *for* / *since* we were young.
5 It's been much warmer *for* / *since* the rain stopped.
6 She's only had that toy *for* / *since* three weeks.

2 Make sentences with the Present perfect and *for* or *since*.

1 Jared / not write / to his parents / March.
Jared hasn't written to his parents since March.
2 You / watch / that show / hours!
....
3 Maria / live here / two years.
....
4 The weather / be / very hot / the 15th.
....
5 We / not stay / in a hotel / October.
....
6 Pablo / have to / stay in bed / five days.
....
7 I / not put up / a tent / last summer.
....

3 **Choose the correct options.**

1 How *long* / *many* have you had your laptop?
2 How *long* / *many* days have you had a cold?
3 How *long* / *many* has Jane been in France?
4 How *long* / *many* times have you visited the museum?
5 How *long* / *many* have we had to wait?
6 How *long* / *many* letters have you sent?

4 **Make questions for the underlined answers.**

1 My mom has made four cakes for the party.
How many cakes has your mom made for the party?
2 He's had to walk to school since the beginning of the month.
....
3 I've worked here for six weeks.
....
4 We've been abroad three times.
....
5 Your dad's been at the airport for three hours!
....
6 We've had our new car since last April.
....

• Past simple with *just*

5 **Match the questions (1–6) to the answers (a–f).**

1 Where are the postcards? *c*
2 Is Kathy at home?
3 Am I in time for the movie?
4 Is dinner ready?
5 Do you have my keys?
6 Are you ready to go?

a I just put them back on the shelf.
b Yes! It just started.
c I just mailed them.
d Yes! We just packed our bags.
e No. She just left.
f Your dad just put it on the table!

6 **Put the words in the correct order.**

1 He's feeling happy because / good / he / news / got / just / some
He's feeling happy because he just got some good news.
2 She's feeling great because / test / passed / just / she / her
....
....
3 Mom's still a little sleepy because / woke / just / she / up
....
....
4 My sister's really excited because / planned / she / a / just / vacation
....
....
5 Tim's tired because / kilometers / walked / he / just / ten
....
....
6 I feel really good because / went / I / just / to / the / gym
....
....
7 Andy's laughing because / good / heard / he / just / a / joke
....
....

Grammar Reference 6

• Have to/Don't have to

Affirmative
I/You/We/They have to set the table. He/She/It has to set the table.
Negative
I/You/We/They don't have to set the table. He/She/It doesn't have to set the table.
Questions and short answers
Do you have to do any chores? Yes, I do./No, I don't. Does he have to do any chores? Yes, he does./No, he doesn't.

Use

- We use *have to* when there is an obligation to do something.
  *I'm sorry, but we **have to leave** now.*
- We use *don't have to* when there is no obligation.
  *You **don't have to come** if you don't want to.*

• Must/Mustn't

Affirmative and negative		
I/You/He/She/It We/They	must listen	to her.
I/You/He/She/It We/They	mustn't (must not) listen	to her.

Use

- We use *must* when there is an obligation to do something.
  *You **must take** your medicine now!*
  *In the US, you **must drive** on the right.*
- We use *mustn't* to express prohibition— an obligation NOT to do something.
  *You **mustn't wear** shoes inside the house.*
  *You **mustn't take** photographs inside the museum.*

• Predictions with *will, won't, might*

Definite
I think she'll be relieved. You won't have any problems, I'm sure. Will they finish it?
Possible
I might see them tomorrow. I'm not sure. He might not like the movie.

Use

- We use *will/won't* to express what we think of as a definite future.
  *I'm sure they**'ll be** very happy.*
  *We**'ll** never **forget** you!*
  *There **won't be** much traffic in the morning.*
- We use *might* to express what we think of as only possible, but not definite.
  *If you're here tomorrow, I **might see** you in the library.*
  *We **might not go** out if the weather's bad.*

Grammar practice • Have to/Don't have to, must/mustn't

1 Make sentences with the correct form of *have to/don't have to.*

1 Sue can't go out because she / have / study.
Sue can't go out because she has to study.

2 What chores do I / have to / do next weekend?

....

3 Did you / have to / work late / last night?

....

4 They're staying in a hotel, so they / not have to / cook / meals.

....

5 Do / we / have to / wear / suits for the wedding tomorrow?

....

6 Phil got up early, so I / not have to / wake him up.

....

2 Complete the conversation with the correct form of *have to*.

A What's it like at your summer camp?
B Some things are the same as at home. We [1] *have to* get up early, and we [2]....................... make the bed. But we [3]....................... do all the activities, because we can usually choose.
A That sounds OK! What about meals? [4]....................... (you) cook?
B No, we don't. There's a specific activity in the morning if you want to learn.
A And at night, what time [5]....................... (you) go to bed?
B Officially, we [6]....................... turn off the lights at midnight, but most of us sit and chat in the dark until much later.

3 Life in the army. Look at the table. Write sentences with *mustn't*, *have to/don't have to*. (O = Obligation, N/O = No obligation, P = Prohibition)

1 get up late	P
2 sweep the floors	O
3 wash uniforms	N/O
4 iron uniforms	O
5 cook meals	P
6 get exercise	O
7 speak English	N/O

1 They *mustn't get up late.*
2 They ....
3 They ....
4 They ....
5 They ....
6 They ....
7 They ....

• Predictions with *will, won't, might*

4 Complete the sentences with *will*, *won't* or *might*.

1 Tom is sick, so he *won't* be in class today.
2 The weather is very changeable, so you .... need an umbrella.
3 .... you bring me a souvenir from Sweden?
4 Jessie's in the backyard, so she .... (not) hear you.
5 It has snowed a lot, so it .... take longer to get home today.

5 Write sentences with *will*, *won't* or *might*.

1 I / not think / Shira / go / to the theater. (will)
I don't think Shira will go to the theater.
2 Tamara / be / very upset, / so / she not go out tonight. (won't)
....
....
3 Rob / invite you / to the party / if / you ask him nicely! (might)
....
....
4 Where / you be / at five o'clock / tomorrow afternoon? (will)
....
....
5 Diana / be / very smart, / but / she not know / the answer! (might)
....
....
6 Reggie / look / tired, / but / he not give up! (won't)
....
....

Grammar Reference

• Be going to

Affirmative
There are going to be 200 elephant sculptures. The charity is going to make "elephant corridors."
Negative
There aren't going to be 200 elephant sculptures. The charity isn't going to make "elephant corridors."
Questions and short answers
Are they going to make them? Yes, they are./No, they aren't. What are they going to do?

Use

We use *be going to* in order to express some kind of future intention or plan:

*We**'re going to take** skiing lessons this winter.*

***I'm not going to practice** the piano today because I don't have time.*

• *Will* or *be going to*

Predictions
In 30 years there won't be any Asian elephants. You'll probably meet one in town this weekend.
Plans or intentions
We're going to save the Asian elephant.

Use

We use *will* to express a prediction:

*You**'ll find** the spoons in the drawer next to the stove.*

*Carmen **will** probably **study** chemistry.*

We often use *will* after these expressions:

I think/I don't think, *I'm sure/I'm not sure*, *maybe*, *perhaps*.

• First conditional

if + Present simple, *will* + infinitive
If we don't protest, they will close the library.
***will ('ll)* + infinitive > *if* + Present simple**
They will close the library if we don't protest.

Use

We use the First conditional to talk about possible situations. We feel these situations have a real chance of happening if the condition comes true:

*If you **don't hurry up**, we**'ll miss** the bus.*

*If it **rains** today, we**'ll stay** home.*

Form

If + Present simple, *will* + infinitive:

*If the weather **is** good, we**'ll go** swimming.*

will + infinitive > *if* + Present simple:

*We**'ll go** swimming **if** the weather **is** good.*

Grammar practice • Be going to

1 Put the words in the correct order.

1 **A** going / dinner / are / to / you / have / What / for / ?
What are you going to have for dinner ?
B Probably just some fruit and yogurt.

2 **A** put / Where / mirror / her / going / is / Jane / to / new / ?
....
B I think it's for her bedroom.

3 **A** are / tattoo / you / to / Why / get / going / a / ?
....
B Because tattoos are cool!

4 **A** theater / the / When / going / to / are / they / open / new / ?
....
B Sometime in September, I think.

Will or be going to

2 Choose the correct options.

1 David isn't sure about the bus. Perhaps *he's going to* / *he'll* take the train. (circled: *he'll*)
2 We like this place! *We're going to* / *We'll* stay three more days.
3 Ana has to work just now. Maybe *she's going to* / *she'll* join us later.
4 He just bought the tickets. *They're going to* / *They'll* travel on Monday.
5 They're flying to Mexico. I'm sure *they're going to* / *they'll* have a wonderful time.
6 I'm not feeling very well, so *I'm going to* / *I'll* take an aspirin.

3 Complete the conversation with the correct form of *will* or *going to*.

A What are your plans for the long weekend?
B We [1] *'re going to* have a special dinner with the family.
A What's on the menu?
B I'm sure Mom [2]........................ cook turkey. It's her specialty. But later maybe we [3]........................ have a special dessert, because I'd like to try something different. What about you?
A We [4]........................ travel to Texas to surprise my brother.
B That'll be fun!
A Yes! He's been working very hard and hasn't been able to get home. He [5]........................ be really happy to see us.
B That [6]........................ be nice!

First conditional

4 Make sentences.

1 If you don't practice enough, you / never / play well!
If you don't practice enough, you'll never play well!
2 If we buy one of these, we / get / another one free.
....
....
3 If you open this box, you / find / a surprise inside.
....
....
4 We'll catch the six o'clock bus if / we / be / lucky!
....
....
5 You'll probably find that information if / you / look / on the Internet.
....
....
6 I'll be very surprised if / Steve / not be / at home.
....
....

5 Complete the replies with the correct form of the verbs.

1 **A** What are you laughing about?
B If I *tell* (tell) you, *will you keep* (you/keep) it a secret?
2 **A** I can't do my homework!
B If I .... (help) you, ... (you/take) the dog for a walk?
3 **A** I don't like this food!
B If you .... (not finish) your food, you .... (not get) any dessert!
4 **A** We're leaving tomorrow!
B .... (you/call) me if I .... (give) you my phone number?
5 **A** This house is a mess!
B .... (you/do) the ironing if I .... (vacuum) the floor?
6 **A** Romeo's gone!
B What .... (Juliet/do) if he .... (not come) back?

Grammar Reference 8

• Second conditional

***if* + Past simple, *would ('d)* + infinitive** ***would ('d)* + infinitive > *if* + Past simple**
Affirmative
If I had an ordinary job, I'd be bored.
Negative
If I weren't a stuntwoman, I'd do extreme sports. If I were scared, I wouldn't be a stuntwoman.
Questions and short answers
Would you be happier if you had an ordinary job? Yes, I would./No, I wouldn't.

Use

We use the Second conditional to talk about unlikely/unreal situations. We feel these situations have very little chance of happening because the condition itself is nearly impossible. The Past simple tense expresses this near impossibility.

*If I **had** the money, I'**d buy** a castle.*

*We'**d stay** longer **if** we **had** the time.*

Form

If + Past simple, *would* + infinitive.

*If I **studied** more, I'**d get** better grades.*

would + infinitive *if* + Past simple.

*I'**d get** better grades **if** I **studied** more.*

We use *were* instead of *was* for the verb *be*.

*If **I were** you, I'd buy a new phone.*

*If my house **were** bigger, I would invite all my family to come to dinner.*

• Relative pronouns

It's the place where I play soccer.
She's the woman who was in the car.
That's the cat which was under a car.

Use

We use relative pronouns to identify people/places/things, or to give more information about them:

*That's the guide **who** showed us the city.*

*This is the hotel **where** we stayed.*

*These are the souvenirs **which** we bought for the family.*

*It's an object **which** we use to open doors.* (= a key)

*It's a place **where** you can relax and enjoy yourself.* (= a vacation resort)

*She's the kind of person **who** can tell you a lot of stories.* (= grandma)

Grammar practice • Second conditional

1 Put the words in the correct order.

What would happen if …

1 off / bus / school / at / didn't / the / get / I / ?
I didn't get off the bus at school?

2 Saturdays / to / had / we / go / on / school / to / ?
....

3 with / man / the / spy / newspaper / were / the / a / ?
....

If I didn't take the bus, …

4 bike / school / by / to / go / could / I
....

5 time / get / on / wouldn't / school / to / I
....

6 rain / to / have / would / the / I / to / walk / in / school
....

2 **Make sentences.**

1 If I were you, I / not do that again.
If I were you, I wouldn't do that again.

2 If this story were true, we / all be / in serious trouble!
....
....

3 If Dad saw you now, he / not believe his eyes!
....
....

4 They'd have to go to the hospital if his fever / not go down.
....
....

5 I'd ask for a refund if my flight / be canceled.
....
....

6 I wouldn't believe him if I / not know him!
....
....

3 **Complete the replies with the correct form of the verbs.**

1 **A** So you're going to be late?
B Sorry! If there *were* (be) an earlier train, we*'d get* (get) there in time.

2 **A** Will Uncle Jack remember it's my birthday?
B I .... (be) very surprised if he .... (not send) you a present.

3 **A** I don't know what to do!
B If I .... (be) you, I .... (ask) your father for some ideas.

4 **A** You have too much luggage!
B I know. If I .... (have) a car, it .... (not be) a problem.

5 **A** Can you see the animals over there?
B It .... (be) much easier if there .... (not be) so many trees!

6 **A** Are you enjoying the walk?
B It .... (not be) so difficult if the path .... (not be) so narrow.

• Relative pronouns

4 **Complete the conversation with *who, which,* or *where.***

A Have you seen these photos before?
B No, I haven't.
A Well, this is the classmate [1] *who* had a fever, and had to go home.
B OK. And this?
A That's the science room [2] .... two students got burns in an experiment.
B How did that happen?
A They were using equipment [3] .... didn't work properly.
B Who's that girl there?
A She's the one [4] .... got a rash from touching frogs in biology class.
B Yes, that happened to a friend of mine, too. He played with some cats [5] .... lived near the beach, and his hands went all red.
A Is that the beach [6] .... we were on vacation this summer?
B No. It's a different one.

5 **Make sentences with *who, which* or *where.***

1 This is a photo / the accident / I have / when I / be ten.
This is a photo of the accident which I had when I was ten.

2 This is the park / it happen.
....

3 These are the skates / I be / wearing.
....

4 Here's the doctor / put the cast / on my arm.
....
....

5 This is the café / my father / buy / me an ice cream cone.
....
....

6 This is the nurse / write / a message on my cast.
....
....

Grammar Reference

• Present simple passive

Affirmative
It is made with plastic tubes. They are made with plastic.
Negative
The machine isn't made with plastic. Gloves aren't usually used to climb walls.
Questions and short answers
Is the machine made with plastic? Yes, it is./No, it isn't. Are the gloves used to climb walls? Yes, they are./No, they aren't.

Use

We use the passive when we want to focus more on an action than on the person or thing doing the action:
*Coffee **is produced** in many different countries.*

Form

subject + Present simple of *be* + past participle of the main verb
***Coffee is produced** in tropical countries.*
***Coffee is not produced** in cold countries.*
***Is coffee produced** in Africa? Yes, it is.*

• Past simple passive

Affirmative	Negative
It was made by Ella.	It wasn't made by Ella.
They were bought yesterday.	The instructions weren't included in the box.
Questions and short answers	
Was it made from an aluminum can? Yes, it was./No, it wasn't. Were the instructions included? Yes, they were./No, they weren't.	

Form

subject + Past simple of *be* + past participle of the main verb
***The first cars were made** in the late 1800s.*
***Cars were not built** before the late 1800s.*
***Were the first cars made** in Europe? Yes, they were.*

• Active and passive

Active
Blind people use Braille. You write messages on a keyboard.
Passive
Braille is used by blind people. Messages are written on a keyboard.

Use

We use **active** forms when the person or thing doing the action is important:
Some people in Ireland speak Gaelic.

We use **passive** forms when we consider the action more important than the person or thing doing it:
*Gaelic **is spoken** in Ireland.* (= this is where we find Gaelic spoken)
*Many buildings **were destroyed** in this city.*
(= an important fact)

Sometimes we also want to specify the person or thing doing the action:
*Gaelic **is spoken by some people** in Ireland.*
(= not everyone speaks the language)
*Many buildings **were destroyed by fire**.*
(= fire and not water or other causes)

Most often, however, the person or thing doing the action is not mentioned:
*Video games **are produced** in Japan.*
*Houses in this area **are built** of wood or brick.*

Grammar practice • Present simple passive

1 Complete the sentences with the Present simple passive form of the verbs.

1 Our computers *are packed* (pack) in this department here.
2 The keyboard .... (attach) to the case.
3 The power cords .... (add) in a separate box.
4 The battery .... (produce) in a different factory.

5 The buttons .... (test) by that department there.
6 The remote control .... (sell) separately.

2 Make questions with the Present simple passive.

1 Where / power cords / plug in?
Where are the power cords plugged in?
2 How / this tube / produce?
....
3 What kind of keyboard / use / in China?
....
4 How / the buttons / add?
....
5 When / the battery / attach?
....
6 Where / these engines / build?
....

• Past simple passive

3 Make sentences with the Past simple passive.

1 Horses / domesticate / over 6,000 years ago.
Horses were domesticated over 6,000 years ago.
2 Modern bicycles / not invent / until about 1885.
....
....
3 The first car factory / build / in Germany in 1885.
....
....
4 City bus services / begin / in England and France in the 1820s.
....
....
5 The first railway trains / run in England in the 1820s.
....
....
6 The first airplanes / not fly / until 1903.
....
....

4 Complete the questions with the Past simple passive form of the verbs.

1 When *was* the local theme park *opened*? (open)
2 Where .... the *Twilight* movies .... ? (make)
3 When .... the baby .... to its father in *Ice Age 1*? (return)
4 How .... Princess Fiona .... by Shrek? (rescue)
5 When .... the ring .... into the volcano in *The Lord of the Rings*? (throw)
6 Where .... *High School Musical* .... ? (film)

• Active and passive

5 Change these active sentences into passive sentences. Include *by* + noun only if necessary.

1 People make flour from wheat.
Flour is made from wheat.
2 The school theater group performed this play.
....
....
3 Someone in Canada writes this blog.
....
....
4 The local factory produces one thousand cars a week.
....
....
5 Mark Zuckerberg created a huge social network.
....
....
6 A monkey stole our sandwiches!
....
....
7 Three boys discovered some old coins in a field.
....
....

Vocabulary

Enjoy Your Vacation!

Unit vocabulary

1 Translate the words.

Vacation
book a flight/hotel ....
buy souvenirs ....
check into a hotel ....
eat out ....
get a tan ....
get lost ....
go camping ....
go sightseeing ....
lose your luggage ....
pack your bag ....
put up a tent ....
stay in a hotel ....
take a trip ....
write a travel blog ....

2 Translate the words.

Meanings of *get*
arrive (*get to the campsite*)
....
become (*get cold*) ....
bring (*get the sunscreen*)
....
buy (*get a key ring*)
....
receive (*get a postcard*)
....
walk/move (*get on the bus*)
....

Vocabulary extension

3 Match the photos to these words. Use your dictionary if necessary. Write the words in English and in your language.

book bed and breakfast	buy a travel pass	take a taxi
get sunburned	~~stay at a youth hostel~~	

1 *stay at a youth hostel*
....

2 ....
....

3 ....
....

4 ....
....

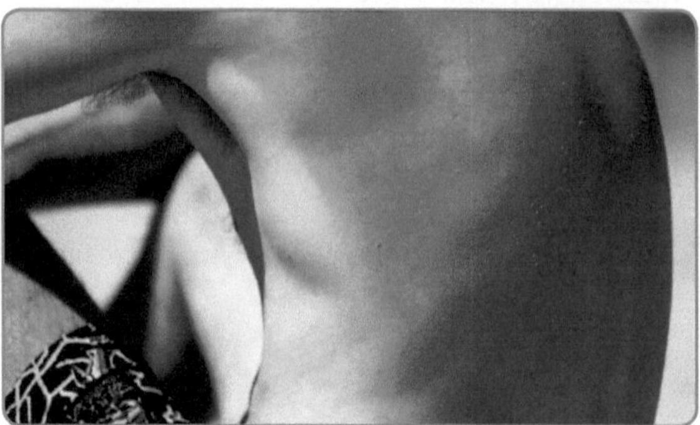

5 ....
....

Vocabulary

That's Life!

Unit vocabulary

1 Translate the words

Household chores

clear the table ....
cook a meal ....
do the dishes ....
do the ironing ....
do the laundry ....
feed the cat ....
hang out the laundry ....
load the dishwasher ....
make your bed ....
mow the lawn ....
set the table ....
sweep the floor ....
take out the trash ....
vacuum the floor ....
walk the dog ....
wash the car ....

2 Translate the words.

Feelings adjectives

confident ....
confused ....
disappointed ....
embarrassed ....
fed up ....
glad ....
grateful ....
guilty ....
jealous ....
lonely ....
nervous ....
relaxed ....
relieved ....
upset ....

Vocabulary extension

3 Match the photos to these words. Use your dictionary if necessary. Write the words in English and in your language.

~~anxious~~	carefree	change the sheets
mop the floor	water the plants	

1 ....
....

2 ....
....

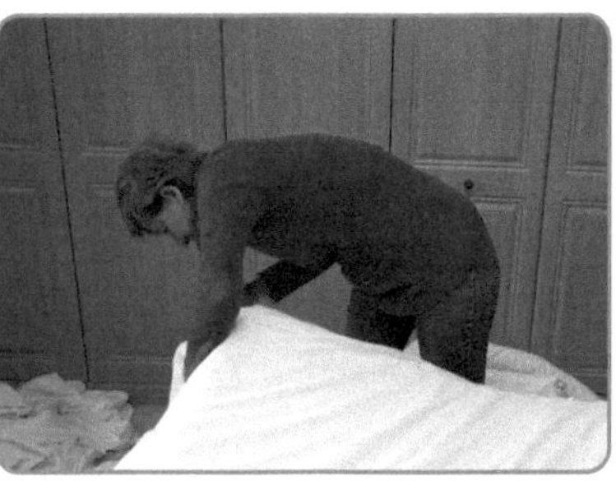

3 ....
....

4 ....*anxious*............
....

5 ....
....

Vocabulary

Make a Difference

Unit vocabulary

1 Translate the words.

Protest and support

banner ....
charity ....
collection ....
demonstration ....
donation ....
fundraising event ....
march ....
petition ....
sign ....
sit-in ....
slogan ....
volunteer ....

2 Translate the words.

Verb + preposition

agree with ....
apologize for ....
argue with ....
believe in ....
care about ....
decide on ....
disapprove of ....
hope for ....
insist on ....
know about ....
protest against ....
worry about ....

Vocabulary extension

3 Match the photos to these words. Use your dictionary if necessary. Write the words in English and in your language.

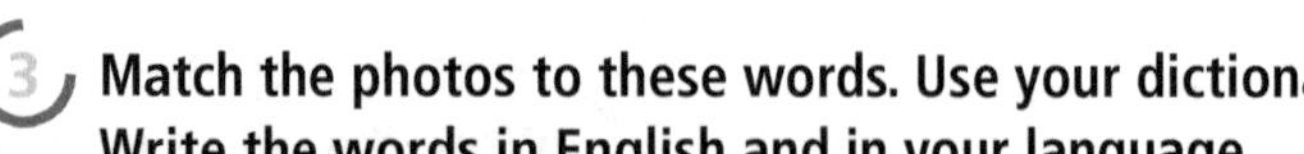

campaign for/against | disaster relief | ~~endangered species~~ | human rights | minority group

1 ....
....

2 ....
....

3  *endangered species*
....

4 ....
....

5 ....
....

Vocabulary

Danger and Risk

Unit vocabulary

1 **Translate the words.**

Extreme adjectives

awful ....
burning ....
excellent ....
exhausted ....
freezing ....
furious ....
huge ....
terrifying ....
thrilled ....
tiny ....

2 **Translate the words.**

Illness and injury

a backache ....
a burn ....
a cold ....
a cough ....
a cut ....
a fever ....
a headache ....
a rash ....
a sore throat ....
a sprained ankle ....
a stomachache ....
a toothache ....

Vocabulary extension

3 **Match the photos to these words. Use your dictionary if necessary. Write the words in English and in your language.**

bandage delighted ~~horrified~~ needle cast

1 ....
....

2 ....*horrified*..........
....

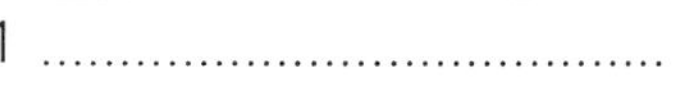

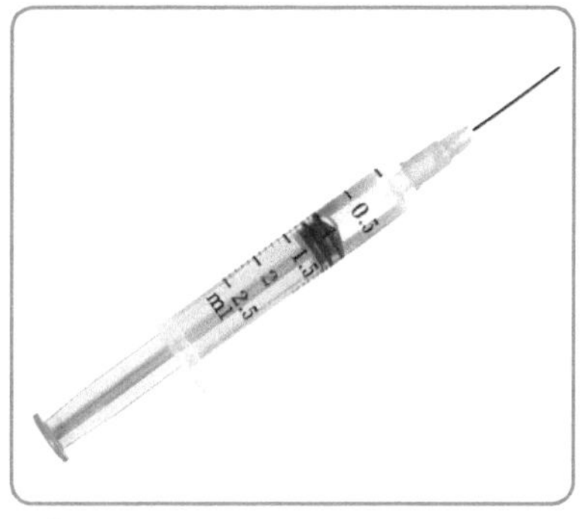

3 ....
....

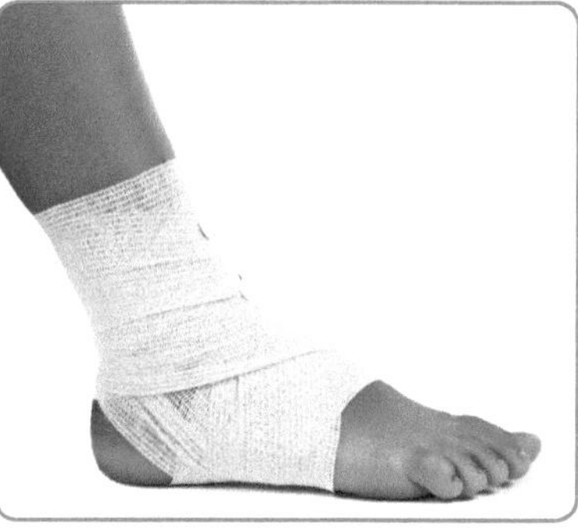

4 ....
....

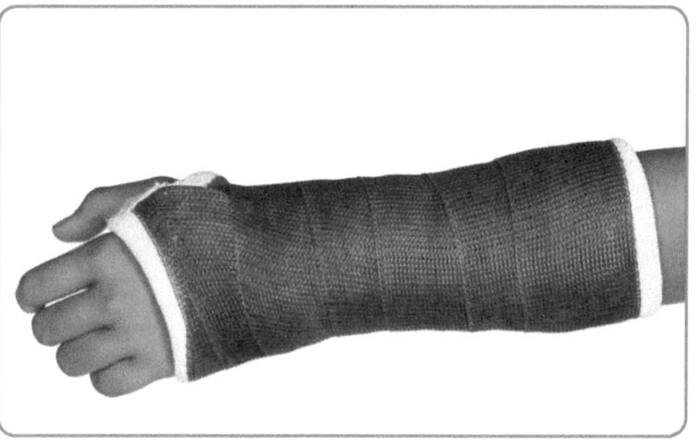

5 ....
....

Vocabulary

Inventions

Unit vocabulary

1 **Translate the words.**

Machine verbs

attach ....
build ....
communicate ....
invent ....
plug in ....
press ....
produce ....
turn on/off ....

Machine nouns

battery ....
button ....
cable ....
jack ....
keyboard ....
outlet ....
power cord ....
remote control ....
tube ....
wheel ....

2 **Translate the words.**

Word building

build – builder – building
....
design – designer – design
....
invent – inventor – invention
....
paint – painter – painting
....
produce – producer – product
....
write – writer – writing
....

Vocabulary extension

3 **Match the photos to these words. Use your dictionary if necessary. Write the words in English and in your language.**

composer | enter key | function key | sale | ~~unplug~~

1 ....*unplug*.............
....

2 ....
....

3 ....
....

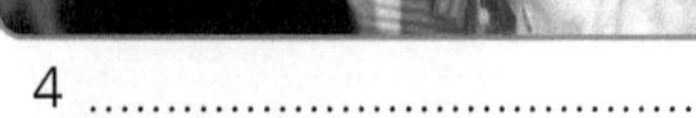

4 ....
....

5 ....
....

Speaking and Listening

Asking for information

• Speaking

1 **Put the words in order. Then listen and check.**
54
A [1] me / Excuse / us / Can / help / you / ! / ?
Excuse me! Can you help us?
B Sure!
A [2] to / T-shirts / good / a / Where's / buy / place / ?
....
B There's a souvenir shop near the station.
A [3] can / there / get / we / And / how / ?
....
B It's a five-minute walk.
A [4] there / money / there / get / a / bank / to / Is / ?
....
B There's one inside the station.
A [5] take / zoo / How / get / does / to / long / it / the / to / ?
....
B About fifteen minutes by bus.

2 **Complete the conversation with these phrases. Then listen and check.**
55

About twenty minutes	~~for a long time~~
here you go	kind of far
not too expensive	over there
The best way	

A Excuse me! Can you help us? We're looking for the zoo.
B The zoo? I haven't been there [1] *for a long time*! Do you have a map?
A Yes, [2]........................ .
B OK, let's see. This is where we are now, and that's the zoo [3]........................ .
A Is it far?
B It's [4]........................, yes.
A How can we get there?
B [5]........................ is probably by bus. There's a bus every quarter of an hour.
A How long does it take?
B [6]........................ .
A Is there a good place to eat at the zoo?
B Yes, there's a cafeteria, and it's [7]........................ .
A Thank you very much. That's really helpful!

• Listening

3 **You will hear four conversations. Match the conversations (1–4) to the topics (a–d).**
56

a the beach ....
b an art gallery *1*
c sunglasses ....
d a theme park ....

4 **Listen again. Are the statements true (T) or false (F)?**
56

Conversation 1
1 Speaker 2 can't answer the question. *T*

Conversation 2
2 Speaker 1 prefers the taxi. ....

Conversation 3
3 Speaker 2 recommends the pharmacy. ....

Conversation 4
4 There's a bus every half hour. ....

Speaking and Listening

Giving advice

• Speaking

1 57 **Put the conversation in the correct order. Then listen and check.**

a What's the matter? Is there anything I can do? *1*
b Well, why don't you look in the car? ....
c Did you come home on the bus yesterday? ....
d Maybe you should check your room. ....
e Good idea! Why didn't I think of that? Thanks! ....
f No, I didn't. My mom drove me home. ....
g I lost Jill's present. She'll be really upset! ....
h I've looked there three times! ....

2 58 **Complete the conversation with these phrases. Then listen and check.**

don't have to	I won't see	Why don't you
you should let	~~you should worry~~	

A You don't look very happy! What's the matter?
B I've found out that Cheryl's having a party, and she hasn't invited me!
A I don't think [1] *you should worry* about that. Other people have parties, too.
B Yes, but Olivia's going, and if I can't go, [2]........................ her!
A OK, I understand. But you [3]........................ go to a party to see her.
B That's true, but our class schedules at school are very different.
A [4]........................ call Cheryl and ask her for an invitation?
B I'd be too embarrassed!
A All right, maybe [5]........................ me ask her then.
B Will you?
A Sure. Anything for a friend!
B Thanks!

• Listening

3 59 **Listen to the conversation. Choose the correct options.**

1 The *boy* / *girl* is fed up. (*girl* circled)
2 The girl has to take care of *her parents'* / *her brother's* dog.
3 She has to *feed and wash* / *feed and walk* the dog.
4 The boy offers the girl *one solution* / *two solutions* to the problem.
5 The boy has a *cat* / *dog*.

4 59 **Listen again. Who says these phrases? Write B for the boy or G for the girl.**

1 What's new with you? *B*
2 What's the matter? ....
3 It's not fair! ....
4 just tell me ....
5 That's great ....

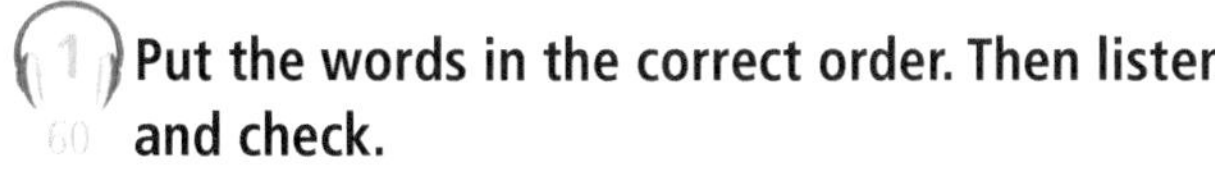

Persuading

• Speaking

1 (60) **Put the words in the correct order. Then listen and check.**

A Let's go and take up a collection. Come on.
[1] fun / It'll / be / !
It'll be fun!
B I'm not so sure about that.

A I don't really want to design banners for you.
B [2] better / It's / doing / nothing / than / !
....

A But we don't know how to make signs.
B [3] can / quickly / sure / we / I'm / learn
....

A What about a petition?
B [4] know / idea / I / if / good / that's / a / don't
....

A I'm sure you'll do a great job.
B [5] it / do / OK, / I'll / !
....

2 (61) **Complete the conversation with these phrases. Then listen and check.**

I don't know	~~If I paint the slogans~~
I'm not sure about	it'll be fun
it's better than	

A We need to make some signs for next weekend!
B Who's "we," Dad?
A You and me, of course.
B But it's your sit-in, Dad. You're organizing it.
A And if I lose my job, you won't get any allowance! [1] *If I paint the slogans*, will you cut the wood?
B [2]........................ , Dad.
A Come on, [3]........................ to work together!
B But you know I'm allergic to sawdust!
A I know that you *say* you're allergic! OK, I'll cut the wood, but you'll have to paint the slogans!
B [4]........................ that.
A Well, [5]........................ walking home after your party tonight, isn't it?
B All right, you win. I'll do it!

• Listening

3 (62) **Listen to the conversation and complete the summary. Use one word in each space.**

The girl wants her mother to go to a [1] *fundraising* event with her. She wants to help a [2]........................ , but her mother doesn't really [3]........................ to go. The mother wants the girl to help her [4]........................ the sheets, but the girl [5]........................ like that idea. In the end, the mother [6]........................ the girl to help, and they both go out together.

4 (62) **Listen again. Who says these phrases? Write M for mother or D for daughter.**

1 a little busy *M*
2 for a charity ....
3 I'll tell you what. ....
4 not good at that ....
5 you'll learn quickly ....

Speaking and Listening

Talking about health

• Speaking

1 Choose the correct options. Then listen and check.
63

1 **A** What's wrong with you?
B My forehead is *burning hot / exhausted*! I think I have a fever.
2 **A** What's the matter with you?
B I feel *exhausted / terrifying*!
3 **A** You don't look well!
B I'm not! I just got a *burn / cold* on my leg!
4 **A** You look awful!
B And I *matter / feel* awful! I have a headache and a bad cough.
5 **A** How do you feel?
B I got up with a terrible backache, but I'm feeling *not too well / a little better* now.

2 Complete the conversation with these phrases. Then listen and check.
64

a little better	~~Are you all right~~
drink some of this	How does it feel
sore throat	

A Hey! [1] *Are you all right*?
B No, I'm not. I have a really [2]...................... .
A Where did you get that?
B I'm not sure. Maybe it was the concert last night.
A Hold on a minute. Here, [3]...................... . That should help you.
B What is it?
A It's something my grandma makes for colds and sore throats. [4]...................... ?
B It tastes really bitter!
A Yes, but what about your throat?
B Oh, that's [5]...................... already, thanks.

• Listening

3 Listen and choose the correct options.
65

1 Andy hurt himself *playing soccer / walking*
2 He got back home by *ambulance / car*.
3 *Andy went to the doctor. / The doctor visited Andy at home.*
4 Andy has to rest for ten *days / weeks*.
5 Trish suggests *going to the movies / watching a movie at home*.

4 Listen again. Put these phrases in the order you hear them.
65

a That was lucky! ....
b How did you get back? ....
c Why not? ....
d Not too well ..*1*..
e Poor thing! ....

Speaking and Listening

Problems with machines

• Speaking

1 66 **Choose the correct options. Then listen and check.**

1 This digital recorder *isn't* / *doesn't* work.
2 I *can't* / *not* listen to the recordings I made.
3 There might be *nothing* / *something* wrong with the battery.
4 Have you *check* / *checked* it?
5 Have you tried *press* / *pressing* the "play" button?
6 You're pressing the *right* / *wrong* button!

2 67 **Complete the conversation with these phrases. Then listen and check.**

~~Did you press~~	Have you checked
I tried that	Let me take a look
something wrong	that doesn't work

A What's the matter?
B I can't change the channels on the TV.
A [1] *Did you press* the right button on the remote control?
B Yes, [2]........................ , but nothing happens, and it was OK yesterday.
A Have you checked the volume control?
B Yes, and [3]........................ either.
A Well, there must be [4]........................ with the remote control then. [5]........................ the batteries?
B Yes! I took them out and put them back in again.
A [6]........................ . Hmm, one of the batteries isn't making contact. Let's press it in better. There you go. Try it again.
B Great! It works! Thanks a lot!

• Listening

3 68 **Listen and choose the correct answers.**

1 The problem with the coffee maker was due to …
a no electricity.
b no coffee.
c no water.
2 The cause of the problem was …
a a visitor.
b a phone call.
c a TV show.
3 The problem lasted between …
a five and ten minutes.
b ten and fifteen minutes.
c ten and twenty minutes.

4 68 **Listen again. Put these phrases in the order you hear them.**

a you're lucky ....
b the coffee pot over there ....
c How did that happen? ....
d the red light on *1*
e That one! ....

Pronunciation

Consonants

Symbol	Example	Your examples
/p/	park	
/b/	big	
/t/	toy	
/d/	dog	
/k/	car	
/g/	good	
/ʧ/	chair	
/dʒ/	jeans	
/f/	farm	
/v/	visit	
/θ/	three	
/ð/	they	
/s/	swim	
/z/	zoo	
/ʃ/	shop	
/ʒ/	television	
/h/	hot	
/m/	map	
/n/	notes	
/ŋ/	sing	
/l/	laptop	
/r/	room	
/y/	yellow	
/w/	watch	

Vowels

Symbol	Example	Your examples
/ɪ/	rich	
/ɛ/	egg	
/æ/	rat	
/ɑ/	job	
/ʌ/	fun	
/ʊ/	put	
/i/	eat	
/eɪ/	gray	
/aɪ/	my	
/ɔɪ/	boy	
/u/	boot	
/oʊ/	note	
/aʊ/	now	
/ɪr/	hear	
/ɛr/	hair	
/ɑr/	star	
/ɔ/	dog	
/ʊr/	tour	
/ɔr/	door	
/ə/	among	
/ɚ/	shirt	

Unit 5 • /aɪ/ vs /ɪ/

1 **Listen and repeat.**
73

1 There'll be bright sunshine in the five islands.
2 The interactive visit begins at six.
3 When I go by bike, I usually arrive on time.
4 It's a pretty little village in Italy.

2 **Put words from Exercise 1 in the correct column.**
73 **Then listen again and check.**

/aɪ/	/ɪ/
bright	*in*
....	....
....	....
....	....
....	....

Unit 6 • /ʌ/ and /yu/

1 **Listen and repeat.**
74

1 My uncle makes beautiful sculptures.
2 There is a ton of music online.
3 There's a long line outside the new museum.
4 I usually get up early and go running on Sundays.

2 **Put words from Exercise 1 in the correct column.**
74 **Then listen again and check.**

/ʌ/	/yu/
uncle	*beautiful*
....	....
....	....
....	....

Unit 7 • Going to

1 **Listen to the recording. Underline the sentences**
75 **where you hear *gonna* instead of *going to*.**

A What are you going to do today?
B I'm going to a demonstration.
A What are you going to do there?
B I'm going to hold a sign and chant slogans.
A Are you going to a restaurant there?
B I'm not going to make plans right now.
A What time are you going to come back?
B I dunno. I'm just going to take it easy.

2 **Listen again and repeat. First A, then B.**
75

Unit 8 • *gh*

1 **Listen and repeat the sentences.**
76

1 He caught eight fish, and that was enough.
2 They didn't laugh because they were frightened.
3 My daughter is sick and coughs a lot.
4 They taught me that "rough" is the opposite of "smooth."

2 **Put words from Exercise 1 with *gh* in the correct**
76 **column. Then listen again and check.**

/f/	silent
enough	*caught*
....	....
....	....
....	....

Unit 9 • /ɪ/ and /i/

1 **Listen and repeat the sentences.**
77

1 Please keep your feet off the table!
2 Don't swim in the river—it's really deep!
3 I'd like three kilos of green peas.
4 If it isn't in there, then I can't think where it is!

2 **Put words from Exercise 1 with the corresponding**
77 **sounds in the correct column. Then listen again and check.**

/ɪ/	/i/
swim	*Please*
....	....
....	....
....	....
....	....
....	....

Irregular Verb List

Verb	Past Simple	Past Participle
be	was/were	been
become	became	become
begin	began	begun
break	broke	broken
bring	brought	brought
build	built	built
buy	bought	bought
can	could	been able
catch	caught	caught
choose	chose	chosen
come	came	come
cost	cost	cost
cut	cut	cut
do	did	done
draw	drew	drawn
drink	drank	drunk
drive	drove	driven
eat	ate	eaten
fall	fell	fallen
feed	fed	fed
feel	felt	felt
fight	fought	fought
find	found	found
fly	flew	flown
forget	forgot	forgotten
get	got	gotten
give	gave	given
go	went	gone/been
have	had	had
hear	heard	heard
hold	held	held
keep	kept	kept
know	knew	known
leave	left	left
lend	lent	lent

Verb	Past Simple	Past Participle
light	lit	lit
lose	lost	lost
make	made	made
mean	meant	meant
meet	met	met
pay	paid	paid
put	put	put
read /rid/	read /rɛd/	read /rɛd/
ride	rode	ridden
ring	rang	rung
run	ran	run
say	said	said
see	saw	seen
sell	sold	sold
send	sent	sent
shine	shone	shone
show	showed	shown
sing	sang	sung
sit	sat	sat
sleep	slept	slept
speak	spoke	spoken
spend	spent	spent
stand	stood	stood
steal	stole	stolen
swim	swam	swum
take	took	taken
teach	taught	taught
tell	told	told
think	thought	thought
throw	threw	thrown
understand	understood	understood
wake	woke	woken
wear	wore	worn
win	won	won
write	wrote	written

My Assessment Profile Unit 5

1 What can I do? Mark (✓) the options in the table.

⏪ = I need to study this again. ⏸ = I'm not sure about this. ▶ = I'm happy with this. ⏩ = I do this very well.

		⏪	⏸	▶	⏩
Vocabulary (pages 4 and 7)	• I can talk about vacations. • I know different meanings of the verb *get*.				
Pronunciation (page 6)	• I can understand and say correctly the sounds /aɪ/ and /ɪ/.				
Reading (pages 5 and 10)	• I can understand stories about travel experiences and tourist attractions.				
Grammar (pages 6 and 9)	• I can use the Present perfect with *for* and *since* correctly. • I can use the Past simple with *just*. • I can ask questions with *How long?*				
Speaking (pages 8 and 9)	• I can ask for information.				
Listening (page 10)	• I can understand a radio show about unusual hotels.				
Writing (page 11)	• I can use adjectives and new vocabulary in my writing. • I can write a travel guide.				

2 What new words and expressions can I remember?

words ....

expressions ....

3 How can I practice other new words and expressions?

record them on my MP3 player ☐ write them in a notebook ☐
practice them with a friend ☐ translate them into my language ☐

4 What English have I learned outside class?

	words	expressions
on the radio		
in songs		
in movies		
on the Internet		
on TV		
with friends		

My Assessment Profile  

1 What can I do? Mark (✓) the options in the table.

(◀◀) = I need to study this again. (II) = I'm not sure about this. (▶) = I'm happy with this. (▶▶) = I do this very well.

		◀◀	II	▶	▶▶
Vocabulary (pages 14 and 17)	• I can talk about household chores. • I can use adjectives to describe feelings.				
Pronunciation (page 17)	• I can understand and say correctly the sounds /ʌ/ and /yu/.				
Reading (pages 15 and 20)	• I can understand articles about household chores.				
Grammar (pages 16, 17 and 19)	• I can use verbs to express obligation, no obligation and prohibition correctly. • I can make predictions with *will*, *won't* and *might*.				
Speaking (pages 18 and 19)	• I can give advice.				
Listening (page 20)	• I can understand conversations between teenagers of the future.				
Writing (page 21)	• I can explain reasons and results. • I can write a letter of advice.				

2 What new words and expressions can I remember?

words ....

expressions ....

3 How can I practice other new words and expressions?

record them on my MP3 player ☐ write them in a notebook ☐
practice them with a friend ☐ translate them into my language ☐

4 What English have I learned outside class?

	words	expressions
on the radio		
in songs		
in movies		
on the Internet		
on TV		
with friends		

My Assessment Profile Unit

1 What can I do? Mark (✓) the options in the table.

⏪ = I need to study this again. ⏸ = I'm not sure about this. ▶ = I'm happy with this. ⏩ = I do this very well.

		⏪	⏸	▶	⏩
Vocabulary (pages 28 and 31)	• I can talk about protest and support. • I can use verbs with prepositions.				
Pronunciation (page 30)	• I can hear the difference between *gonna* and *going to.*				
Reading (pages 29 and 34)	• I can understand articles about protest and support issues.				
Grammar (pages 30, 31 and 33)	• I can use *be going to* and *will* correctly. • I can use the First conditional.				
Speaking (pages 32 and 33)	• I can persuade someone to do something.				
Listening (page 34)	• I can understand an interview about a charity.				
Writing (page 35)	• I can format a letter or email correctly. • I can write a formal letter.				

2 What new words and expressions can I remember?

words ....

expressions ....

3 How can I practice other new words and expressions?

record them on my MP3 player ☐ write them in a notebook ☐

practice them with a friend ☐ translate them into my language ☐

4 What English have I learned outside class?

	words	expressions
on the radio		
in songs		
in movies		
on the Internet		
on TV		
with friends		

My Assessment Profile Unit 8

1 What can I do? Mark (✓) the options in the table.

⏪ = I need to study this again. ⏸ = I'm not sure about this. ▶ = I'm happy with this. ⏩ = I do this very well.

		⏪	⏸	▶	⏩
Vocabulary (pages 38 and 41)	• I can use extreme adjectives. • I can talk about illness and injury.				
Pronunciation (page 41)	• I can hear the difference between *gh* with the sound /f/ and silent *gh*.				
Reading (pages 39 and 44)	• I can understand articles about danger and risk.				
Grammar (pages 40 and 43)	• I can use the Second conditional correctly. • I can use relative pronouns.				
Speaking (pages 42 and 43)	• I can talk about health.				
Listening (page 44)	• I can understand a conversation about an adventure game show.				
Writing (page 45)	• I can interpret an application form. • I can fill in an application form correctly.				

2 What new words and expressions can I remember?

words ....

expressions ....

3 How can I practice other new words and expressions?

record them on my MP3 player ☐ write them in a notebook ☐

practice them with a friend ☐ translate them into my language ☐

4 What English have I learned outside class?

	words	expressions
on the radio		
in songs		
in movies		
on the Internet		
on TV		
with friends		

My Assessment Profile Unit 9

1 What can I do? Mark (✓) the options in the table.

⏪ = I need to study this again. ⏸ = I'm not sure about this. ▶ = I'm happy with this. ⏩ = I do this very well.

		⏪	⏸	▶	⏩
Vocabulary (pages 48 and 51)	• I can talk about machines. • I can use machine-related nouns and verbs.				
Pronunciation (page 51)	• I can understand and say correctly the sounds /ɪ/ and /i/.				
Reading (pages 49 and 54)	• I can understand articles about machines and inventions.				
Grammar (pages 50 and 53)	• I can use the Present simple passive and Past simple passive correctly. • I know when to use *by* in passive sentences.				
Speaking (pages 52 and 53)	• I can talk about problems with machines.				
Listening (page 54)	• I can understand a conversation about the advantages and disadvantages of reading on a smart phone.				
Writing (page 55)	• I can organize an opinion essay. • I can write an opinion essay with reasons and examples.				

2 What new words and expressions can I remember?

words ....

expressions ....

3 How can I practice other new words and expressions?

record them on my MP3 player ☐ write them in a notebook ☐

practice them with a friend ☐ translate them into my language ☐

4 What English have I learned outside class?

	words	expressions
on the radio		
in songs		
in movies		
on the Internet		
on TV		
with friends		

Notes

Notes

Notes

Notes

Notes

Notes

Pearson Education Limited
Edinburgh Gate
Harlow
Essex CM20 2JE
England
and Associated Companies throughout the world.

www.pearsonelt.com/moveit

First published 2015
Seventh impression 2024

Set in 10.5/12.5pt LTC Helvetica Neue Light
ISBN: 978-1-2921-0136-1

Printed and bound by CPI Group (UK) Ltd, Croydon CR0 4YY

Acknowledgements

We are grateful to the following for permission to reproduce copyright material:
Article 1.1 adapted from www.minihousebuilder.com; Article 6.7 adapted from www.bullyingcanada.ca

Photo Acknowledgements

The publisher would like to thank the following for their kind permission to reproduce their photographs:

(Key: b-bottom; c-centre; l-left; r-right; t-top)

Students' Book:
akg-images Ltd: 54tr, Erich Lessing 54cl; **Alamy Images:** AE / Gunter Marx 38t, Colin Palmer Photography 68tr, Ashley Cooper 28c, Design Pics Inc 28bl, Bert Hoferichter 70bl, Impressions / Balan Madhavan 29l, Picture Contact BV 70br, Evan Spiler 66r, ZUMA Press, Inc 29r; **Bridgeman Art Library Ltd:** Arundel Castle 54cr; **Bullying Canada :** Charles Benn 23r; **Crina Coco Popescu:** 47l, 47r; **Corbis:** Destinations 5tr, epa / Jerry Lampen 44l, Leonard Gertz 64br/8, Minden Pictures / Foto Natura / Do Van Dijck 64br/7, Ocean 15r, Pool / Retna Ltd 30r, Reuters / Peter Andrews 10tr; **Divine Chocolate:** 37tr, Kim Naylor 37tl; **Dynamic Graphics, Inc.:** 70tr; **Fotolia.com:** Aaron Amat 64br/6, dell 22, Patryk Kosmider 67r, Miravision 12, Anna Omelchenko 64br/2, Scanrail 55, Petr Vaclavek 54tl; **Getty Images:** 28t, 28cl, 28br, 66l, AFP 10cr, 38c, Todd Bigelow 10cl, Scott Cramer 38b, National Geographic 49l (Bkgd), Simon Rawles 37b, Kenneth Riley 13b, Henrik Sorensen 64br/1, Yellow Dog Productions 21; **Pearson Education Ltd:** Gareth Boden 8, 18, 32, 42, 52, 62tl, 62tr, 63bl, 64tl, 64tr, 65l; **Press Association Images:** Demotix / Clive Chilvers 28cr; **Reuters:** Karoly Arvai 34r; **Rex Features:** 60, Robert Harding / Charles Bowman 68tl, Geoffrey Robinson 49cl/a, Universal / Everett 68br; **Jorge Rodriguez-Gerada:** 34l; **Shutterstock.com:** 40, Lance Bellers 59, BestPhotoStudio 31, 58, Brandon Blinkenberg 70cr, Jaimie Duplass 6, Warren Goldswain 5bl, gudak 49bl/b, Kamira 69c, Stuart Monk 69r, PhotoHouse 69l, Dmitriy Shironosov 26; **SuperStock:** age fotostock / Mark Beton 11, age fotostock / Werner Otto 64br/5, Aurora Open / Tom Bol 5cr, Image Source 15l, OJO Images 64br/4, Oredia / Oredia Eurl / Antoine Juliette 64br/3; **The Kobal Collection:** Warner Bros 39; **TopFoto:** The Granger Collection 54br; **www.StopBullying.gov:** 23l

Workbook:
Alamy Images: Mark Boulton 130cr, Cliff Hide News 135, Ashley Cooper 101, Ian Dagnall 114c, Gallo Images 87, Nikolay Mihalchenko 129cr, Mode Images 82, NielsVK 109, redsnapper 137, Andre Seale 115, Colin Underhill 130tl, vario images GmbH & Co.K 77, way out west photography 128tr; **Bridgeman Art Library Ltd:** The Yellow House, 1888 (oil on canvas), Gogh, Vincent van (1853-90) / Van Gogh Museum, Amsterdam, The Netherlands 80; **Corbis:** cultura / Nancy Honey 132b; **Fotolia.com:** 141-145; **FotoLibra:** Nicola Mary Barranger 129cl; **Getty Images:** Cultura / Ghislain & Marie David de Lossy 128cr, Digital Vision / Alistair Berg 129b, Taxi / Javier Pierini 88, Lifesize / John Howard 129tr, Stone / Art Wolfe 130tr, The Image Bank / Larry Dale Gordon 136; **Pearson Education Ltd:** Gareth Boden 112; **Press Association Images:** AP / Leanne Italie 98; **Rex Features:** Image Broker 114t; **Science Photo Library Ltd:** Sinclair Stammers 128b; **Shutterstock.com:** alanf 81, Yuri Arcurs 132cr, Bambuh 131cl, Stacy Barnett 131b, Lance Bellers 128tl, Blend Images 131tl, CandyBox Images 129tl, Hung Chung Chih 130cl, Edw 134, Anton Gvozdikov 105, hansenn 106, Lakeview Images 130b, Petr Malyshev 114b, michaeljung 75, Monkey Business Images 93, oksana2010 131cr, Lana Smirnova 128cl, Tristan Tan 133; **SuperStock:** Zefa 110; **Veer / Corbis:** Adrian Britton 132tl, Roman Ivaschenko 132cl, JohnKwan 132tr, smithore 131tr

Cover images: *Front:* **Shutterstock.com**: Galina Barskaya

All other images © Pearson Education

Every effort has been made to trace the copyright holders and we apologise in advance for any unintentional omissions. We would be pleased to insert the appropriate acknowledgement in any subsequent edition of this publication.

Illustrated by

Students' Book:
Andy Robert Davies; Paula Franco; Peskimo; Zara Picken; Gary Rose; Ben Steers.

Workbook:
Moreno Chiacchiera; Peskimo; Paula Franco